THE HUMAN IMPACT OF NATURAL DISASTERS

ISSUES FOR THE INQUIRY-BASED CLASSROOM

Edited by

VALERIE OOKA PANG, WILLIAM R. FERNEKES AND **JACK L. NELSON**

SCHOOL OF EDUCATION
CURRICULUM LABORATORY
UM-DEARBORN

NCSS
Bulletin 110

National Council for the Social Studies

8555 Sixteenth Street • Suite 500 • Silver Spring, Maryland 20910

www.**socialstudies**.org

Editorial staff on this publication: Michael Simpson, Chi Yang, Jennifer Bauduy, Steven Lapham
Design/Production: Gene Cowan

Library of Congress Control Number: 2010932752
ISBN: 978-0-87986-104-9

Printed in the United States of America
5 4 3 2 1

This Bulletin is dedicated to Gerry, Sheila, and Gwen.
We are grateful for their continuing support.

ACKNOWLEDGEMENT

We acknowledge the contributions of Susan Warner and Save the Children International, who have generously provided the photos included in this Bulletin. We also would like to thank Petra Winiger and Jan Hessbruegge, members of the office for the Representative of the Secretary General on the Human Rights of Internally Displaced Persons, Office of the High Commissioner for Human Rights, for their work in preparing the chapter on protecting human rights.

ON THE COVER

A young woman walks with her bicycle amidst the rubble in the ruins of Han Wang, Sichuan province, China, after the province was hit by an earthquake in 2004. Official figures confirm that 34,000 people died. Save the Children worked closely with the government and the local Red Cross to help with education and child protection in the aftermath of the earthquake. (Colin Crowley/ Save the Children)

TABLE OF CONTENTS

FOREWORD

FELISA TIBBITTS

THE ARTICLES IN THIS NCSS BULLETIN are intended to assist educators in investigating the human impact of natural disasters. The editors and authors analyze these disasters through the lens of human rights and highlight the opportunities to offer human rights education in these challenging contexts.

The Bulletin analyzes several dimensions of natural disasters, including:

- The ways in which humans contribute to their occurrence, thus potentially rendering the impacts of natural disasters more manageable or preventable. The first three chapters address this theme, dealing with "Natural Disasters and Human Rights," "Disasters: Past, Present and Future," and "A Geographic Perspective on Natural Disasters."
- The consequences of natural disasters for the physical and mental well-being of individuals. Chapter 4 discusses "The Psychological Impact of Natural Disasters in School."
- The stress that such disasters place on countries that must address the overwhelming needs of internally displaced persons and refugees (See, for example, Chapter 5 on "Disasters as Threats to Peace" and Chapter 8 on "Poverty and Natural Disasters in Nepal.")

The case studies in Part Two examine disasters in different parts of the world—Haiti, New Orleans, Nepal, Southern Africa and Bangladesh, and review their causes and consequences. A common focus of these articles is the human rights of victims. The disasters have a disproportionate impact on impoverished populations (as Chapters 6, 7 and 8 on Haiti, New Orleans, and Nepal, point out), and can have a particularly devastating effect on women (as Chapter 9 on Southern Africa describes). In some cases, the response to disasters has led to encouraging innovations: Chapter 10 reviews the work of Muhammad Yunis to assist the poor in Bangladesh, a country that has experienced many emergency situations. Part Three of the Bulletin is devoted specifically to examining the human rights of populations who are most severely affected by natural disasters, including internally displaced persons (Chapter 11), people with disabilities (Chapter 12), and children (Chapter 13). In addition to this section, a human rights-based approach (HRBA) serves as a thematic thread connecting the different articles in this Bulletin. The application of human rights is a legal commitment undertaken by parties to the UN Charter and was reaffirmed in 1997 by the UN system as a whole in its Programme of Reform. HRBA applies to all institutions, from the UN Development Programme to the World Bank. A wide range of international actors have made explicit their legal and policy commitment to base their work on human rights, which is now the case for bilateral donor states as well as leading non-governmental organizations (NGOs) active in development and humanitarian response.

HRBA's programming components combine attention to human rights standards with attention to program processes and goals carried out in accordance with the principles of equality and non-discrimination, participation and empowerment, and accountability and rule of law.

Human rights standards are the treaties that a country has signed and ratified and is thus obliged to fulfill from a legal point of view. Independent of these legally binding treaties, the foundational human rights principles of the Universal Declaration of Human Rights (UDHR) are seen by many human rights experts as having the power of customary law, which would mean that governments have the obligation to realize the full set of human rights presented in the UDHR, regardless of the human rights treaties technically in effect. This would be especially true in a situation of mass violation of human rights in the wake of a natural disaster.

This Bulletin illustrates how human suffering following a natural disaster can be categorized as both the failure to protect economic and social human rights (such as the right to housing, the right to water, the right to education, and the right to work) and the failure of states to guarantee civil and political rights (Chapter 11). These are interesting and challenging topics for the U.S. educator to address with students, and they are subjects that go beyond a traditional treatment of the consequences of natural disaster.

A human rights-based approach encourages us not only to analyze the human condition in terms of the degree of realization of individual human rights, but also to consider the root causes of human rights violations. In other words, rather than examining only the consequences of natural disasters, an HRBA analysis would have us investigate the underlying reasons why such events take place in order to understand who is responsible ("duty bearers") for reducing the occurrence of these violations of the rights of "rights holders." This perspective, once again, brings an added dimension to classroom teaching—one that asks learners to consider the origins of natural disasters and ways in which human action can try to prevent human suffering.

Human rights principles are another component of the human rights-based approach. These are a compelling, normative framework for the conduct of programs related to both the prevention and the treatment of the results of natural disasters. HRBA-influenced humanitarian responses should be carried out in ways that help to ensure that the most vulnerable have their human rights protected, promoted, and fulfilled.

Natural disasters bring to light the needs of victims and present opportunities for teachers to educate from a human rights perspective. Chapters 14-16 in Part 4 of the Bulletin deal specifically with educational initiatives and resources, and several other chapters include teaching suggestions and class activities. I am sure that readers will benefit enormously from this unique examination of the humanitarian, political, geographical, and sociological implications of natural disasters—on individuals, groups, and countries. I hope that in considering these complex interactions in our classrooms, we emerge with greater clarity about the ways in which the human rights framework can help us in emphasizing the importance of taking long-term responsibility in preventing natural disasters and organizing relief in a way that respects the full human dignity of all those involved. 🕮

PART 1
DISASTERS AND THEIR IMPACT

CHAPTER 1

NATURAL DISASTERS AND HUMAN RIGHTS: AN INTRODUCTION

JACK L. NELSON, WILLIAM R. FERNEKES, AND VALERIE OOKA PANG

THE STUDY OF NATURAL DISASTERS provides educators with valuable information to understand and deal with past, present and future events. It also enables us to develop more awareness of the human rights issues raised by disastrous events. The study of disasters is important for social studies education for many reasons, including:

- ▶ The significant connection between disasters and human activities
- ▶ The role of disasters in threatening health systems, in increasing armed conflict, in posing threats to human rights, in producing higher levels of poverty, and in the displacement of millions of people throughout the world
- ▶ Social interest in improved knowledge and communications regarding disaster warnings, avoidance, mitigation, and relief
- ▶ Political and economic issues related to damage and recovery
- ▶ Psychological and sociological factors involved in individual, group, and agency actions and reactions
- ▶ Other historical and social scientific academic interests in large-scale events
- ▶ The important focus in social education on the study of social issues
- ▶ The interconnections of science and society

The Human Dimension of Disasters

The study of disaster avoidance, protection, and response requires an examination of human interactions with the environment. Human actions are sometimes the direct cause of disasters: for example, arsonists in Australia created the historic bushfires of 2009, killing hundreds of people and animals, and destroying entire towns. Human actions often also contribute to the scale of disasters. In New Orleans, construction and desertification destroyed natural existing barriers to hurricanes and exacerbated the damage from Hurricane Katrina in 2005; the governmental response to Katrina, with its many failures, was also a human enterprise. The Gulf oil spill in 2010 is another obvious example of a disaster resulting from human actions.

Differences among nations in construction codes, actual buildings, infrastructure, governmental stability, and economic status are also significant factors in protecting people against disasters and responding quickly to them. The impact of these social differences is illustrated by comparing Haiti and Chile in regard to the casualties, damage, and recovery from major earthquakes in 2010. The Haitian quake in January measured 7.0 on the Richter scale, while Chile's in February measured 8.8. Both nations suffered significant casualties and damage, but Haiti's was far worse. The Haitian government determined that about 215,000-230,000 people died; 300,000 were injured; and about 3,000,000 were directly affected by the quake. The limited central governmental infrastructure did not function after the natural disaster, making the relief situation even more dire. In Chile, early estimates had about 700 deaths, though the actual count is closer to 500, and about 2 million were displaced by the quake. Property damage in Haiti is estimated to be as much as $200 billion—in Chile, damage is estimated to be much less. The stark comparison between the earthquakes in Haiti and Chile is an excellent example of how human structures, both physical and social, can determine the extent of damage caused by natural disasters.

Actions by individuals, governments, nongovernmental groups like charities, and international organizations like the United Nations (UN) and the World Bank can create, expand, limit, and react to disasters. Some argue that humans have increasingly created disaster conditions, and cite global warming as one example.[1]

The response of communities and governments to disaster is commonly related to their concepts of justice; this leads to a powerful connection to human rights. As the idea of human rights has expanded, those who are concerned about justice in human events question how societies prepare for and treat those who may create, handle, or suffer from disasters. Who should be protected from danger or damage and why? What personal and property rights should exist in the face of disastrous events?

Which rights are in conflict as a result of disaster conditions related to security, emergency work, looting, commercialization of available resources, privacy, health, poverty, freedom, and accountability? How are group rights (such as those of children, disabled, aged, gender, nationality, and religion) affected by disaster protection and reaction?[2]

The concepts of human and group rights, and the best means of implementing them, are necessarily subject to interpretation. Cultures and subcultures vary in their interpretations of rights for all and for individuals. People in various geographic settings, religious traditions, historic patterns, and relative positions of power hold diverse expectations about rights. Some members of marginalized groups may even accept a view that broad human rights do not apply to them, or only apply in certain conditions. Thus, women in some cultures may not support the granting of full independence to all women; some in the lowest or highest economic strata of many nations may have similar views about the unacceptability of equality of rights. Protection and enforcement of rights is always a matter of judgment, an inexact science in all cultures. Cultural differences deserve consideration in a discussion of how disasters affect rights; this Bulletin, however, bases the discussion on rights identified or supported in the UN Declaration of Human Rights and other relevant international documents. Readers should be cognizant of the views of others whose history, traditions, and experiences may differ from their own.

The complex and subtle intersection between natural disasters and human rights is a major focus of this NCSS Bulletin. The authors explore many of those complexities and provide curricular and instructional ideas for social education about disasters and human rights. Obviously, a single volume cannot contain adequate information on all forms of natural disaster or all varieties of thinking about human rights. Assembled here are a group of topics that illustrate the intersection of these vast realms, with a selection of ideas about educational practice and a collection of resources for more extensive examination.

Defining and Describing Natural Disasters

Identifying disasters appears to be easy. The news media are quick to label them and, by definition, they create large-scale havoc. Although one can call any negative event a disaster—a bad hair day can be disastrous for a job interview—the generally accepted version contemplates extensive damage and disruption to people, places, and things. In Chapter 2, Gunn discusses disaster classification; his two-volume *Encyclopedia of Disasters* offers criteria for defining a disaster to include (1) the number

of people killed, (2) the amount of damage caused, (3) the long-term consequences of the event, and/or (4) some combination of these factors.[3] Using those criteria, Gunn organizes disasters using the following thematic entries:

- ► Earthquakes and Tsunamis
- ► Conflicts
- ► Floods
- ► Human Errors
- ► Hurricanes and Other Tropical Cyclones
- ► Pandemics
- ► Terrorism
- ► Tornadoes
- ► Volcanic Eruptions

This extensive set of categories includes a grouping that might fall outside of consideration in other lists. Human error, for example, includes such events as the mistakes by two workers at Bhopal Chemical Factory in India that led to 8,000 deaths and 250,000 injuries. Terrorism, another human intervention, has more recently been considered a disaster-developer, though terror has been used as a tool for power by governments and renegade groups for centuries.[4]

The scientific effort to recognize and categorize disasters is intended to warn, avoid, mitigate, or eliminate them. The more humans know about natural disasters, the more likely it is that people can act in advance to handle their effects. Early warning depends upon recognition of preliminary factors, like dramatic weather or water temperature changes. Knowledge about earthquakes, wildfires, and hurricanes has led to improved construction and more lead time for preparation. Improved sanitation, the use of immunization, isolation of the sick, and enhanced medical knowledge have been used to control some pandemics, such as the recent H1N1 virus.

Scientific and Social Knowledge

Scientific knowledge often progresses in a broad sequence: identify, classify, predict, and finally, if possible, control phenomena. With regard to disasters, scientists have identified and classified them, have some ability to predict them, but have limited ability to control them. For example, humans now use categories of wind velocity to identify the intensity of hurricanes, and use terms like tropical storm, typhoon, and cyclone to designate wind speed and global location. Communities have increasing understanding of high-wind action and damage from long-term observations on land and in the air, and through computer simulations, and agencies can generate predictions of likely developments. But people are not at a stage of consistently reliable predictions and lack the ability to control natural disasters. Earthquakes, floods, pandemics, and other disasters are works in scientific progress.

While scientific knowledge aims to be precise and exact, social knowledge is more often messy, convoluted, and conflicted. Social knowledge about disasters involves the interaction of science and society, the interaction of disaster knowledge with individual and community lives, the interaction of government and private agencies with communications and operations, and the interaction of social/cultural values with disastrous events. Geographers and other scientists know that building homes on a flood plain in a hurricane-prone area is not scientifically supportable, but it is traditional, economically manageable, and people may prefer the views or location. Property rights and building codes are the result of history, politics, geography, and economics, with some psychology thrown in. In Chapter 3, Pisarra explains how humans have utilized geographical data and not always made the best choices. Local areas and states have emergency plans and voluntary/mandatory conditions for dealing with disasters, but the politics, economics, and psychology of actually implementing them involve factors like individual interests, property considerations, unintended consequences, religious and cultural differences, and the competence of relief managers and workers. These conditions can create confusing or conflicting scenarios in advance of and in response to disasters. Integrating both scientific knowledge and social knowledge in regard to natural disasters often leads to the need to consider human rights.

Considering Human Rights

Human rights are statements of universal applicability to all humans—in short, as Ishay has written, they are "rights held by individuals simply because they are part of the human species... [and] shared equally by everyone regardless of sex, race, nationality and economic background."[5] Rooted in earlier discussions of natural law and the humanistic tenets of major religions, the development of modern conceptions of human rights constitutes a broad expansion beyond the nineteenth century conception that only states were the proper subjects of international law. As Weissbrodt notes, such a view "meant that individuals had no international legal status."[6] But with the development of reform movements that challenged this state-oriented approach, such as the anti-slavery crusade, the development of humanitarian organizations and laws to protect the victims of armed conflicts, the recognition of the right to self-determination, and most importantly, the creation of the United Nations in response to the horrors of World War II and the Holocaust, the development of a universal framework for the protection of human rights that was not predicated on state action came to fruition. Since the adoption of the Universal Declaration of Human Rights (UDHR) by the UN General Assembly in 1948, the United Nations and other international organizations (such as the Organization of American States, European Union, and African Union) have produced a broad range of international treaties and related institutions that elaborate on the statements about fundamental rights made in the UDHR, while seeking to realize the promise of those rights as a commonplace aspect of daily life around the world.

Human rights are also universal in the sense that they constitute "ideal standards" or norms of conduct to which individuals, groups, and states should adhere. Donnelly carefully points out that with a handful of exceptions (the United States often being one of the most glaring examples), over 75% of the world's states "have undertaken international legal obligations to implement these rights by becoming parties to the International Human Rights Covenants, and almost all other nations have otherwise expressed approval of and commitment to their content."[7] Such "international normative universality," to use Donnelly's phrase, has made the promulgation and defense of international human rights guarantees since the mid-20th century a central focus of diplomacy, foreign relations, and public policy development and implementation. More recently, the centrality of human rights considerations in educational policy and practices, gender relations, economic and trade relations, the treatment of children and other special populations (the disabled, refugees, and indigenous peoples are some examples) has strengthened the normative function of human rights worldwide.

In this Bulletin, the intersection of human rights with natural disasters rests not only in their universal applicability to all humans impacted by disasters across the globe, but in the degree to which international norms of conduct have been applied to protect the universal rights of those individuals and groups impacted by natural disasters. This implies that any study of the relationship between human rights and natural disasters has a moral dimension, one that compels the reader to recognize that such a study cannot rest solely on the provision of elemental human needs such as sustenance and safety, but, rather, must include a conception of human possibility that permits every individual to live a life of dignity. Donnelly summarizes this perspective concisely: "Human rights theories and documents point beyond actual conditions of existence—beyond the 'real' in the sense of what has already been realized—to the possible, which is viewed as a deeper human moral reality. Human rights are less about the way people 'are' than about what they might 'become'".[8] Thus Crocco and Chandler's examination of the U. S. government's response to Hurricane Katrina in Chapter 7 highlights not only the failure to provide for basic human needs, but the extent to which individuals who suffered from this immense disaster were denied fundamental rights to a dignified existence, and the degree to which actions of the state have continued to limit the realization of those rights. Similarly, Norman writes in Chapter 4 about how to deal with the impact of disasters on mental health; Lord and Stein explain the impact of disasters on people with disabilities in Chapter 12; and Fernekes deals with disasters and the rights of children in Chapter 13. These contributions focus on efforts to ensure guaranteed rights for vulnerable populations and the gaps that remain between normative standards and actual policies and practices. As an example, the aftermath of the Haitian earthquakes of 2010 has had severe repercussions on the delivery of education to children in that country, where many children have been displaced, living on the streets under the threat of violence, particularly rape.[9] In Chapter 11, Representative Kälin discusses how natural disasters have led to millions being displaced and the resulting poverty that often impacts highly vulnerable populations. Subedi, in Chapter 8, writes about the destabilizing impact of natural disasters in Nepal, where historic inequalities in the distribution of power and wealth, and limited planning to mitigate the effect of such crises have devastating effects on the population.

In Chapter 5, Helsing describes the threats that disasters can pose to political and social stability, citing examples from Darfur, Pakistan, and around the world. He also examines the role of nongovernmental organizations (NGOs) in the rebuilding process. In Chapter 9, Mhlauli, Vosburg-Bluem, and Merryfield discuss how disasters have imposed serious hardship on poor women in southern Africa. Their piece presents inspirational stories of women who have met those challenges and created new lives for themselves and others by creating strong cooperatives.

It is no longer feasible or desirable to maintain the traditional distinctions between civil/political and economic, social, and cultural rights, particularly when case studies of natural or human-made disasters and their impact on the quality of daily life call into question those distinctions. The United Nations Human Development Report in 2000 made a compelling case that human development and human rights are inextricably linked; in short, that "while human rights are ultimately matters of individual entitlement, their fulfillment depends on appropriate social conditions."[10] When natural or human-made disasters

strike and impact the conditions that make human development possible (for example, destroying infrastructure that supports the maintenance of public education, or severely limiting the delivery of essential human services such as sanitation, clean water, and food), then rights guarantees are directly affected. The manner in which societies prioritize human rights concerns in their response(s) to natural and human-made disasters is a critical topic for examination, particularly the degree to which governments see it as their duty to help humans fulfill their rights, and the actions they take to create the social conditions that make that possible.

Within the social studies, human rights education has historically been somewhat marginal as a core topic of study, although developments since the 1980s have led to greater inclusion of human rights content and concepts curricula within the United States and around the globe. Kniep's global education curricular model for social studies in 1986[11] included human rights as one of four central organizing principles, while the systematic efforts of many non-governmental organizations and the United Nations' World Programme for Human Rights Education to incorporate human rights education as a central component of public schooling are making progress.[12] In the United States, the lack of a centralized curriculum-delivery system and the historic resistance to addressing the full range of universal human rights as central components of public discussion have served as obstacles to its inclusion in the social studies curriculum. Banks' 2001 study[13] of state social studies curricula found that at least 20 of the 50 states included human rights to some degree in state-level curriculum standards and/or frameworks. The key challenges facing the social studies field in this area remain the lack of ongoing dialogue and discussion by educators about the core concepts and questions dealing with human rights (i.e., the tensions arising from the critical stance that human rights education has towards the role of government and other aspects of state power), and the relatively minor significance placed on issues-based education as a central focus in social studies classrooms. It is hoped that the contents of this Bulletin will promote the in-depth consideration of the intersections between natural disasters and human rights concerns, and lead to the development of curricular units for classroom instruction where those linkages are examined in detail.

Social Studies Education:
Natural Disasters and Human Rights
Natural disasters and human rights are each a topic of major interest in social education. The social implications of disasters

and the civic interest in rights questions are significant areas for social studies instruction, whether through study in history, geography, politics, sociology, psychology, anthropology, interdisciplinary social science, or issues courses. History and geography, the study of time and space, are shaped by the human understanding of disasters and interest in rights. Societies are necessarily attuned to how the environment and its physical disruptions influence actions. Similarly, political, anthropological, and psychological concepts of individuals and social interactions are strongly influenced by views of human rights. For the issues educator, the intersection of rights and disasters contains a trove of educational value (e.g., exploration of ethical questions about whose rights should trump and why, and questions about the relative human and financial costs and benefits of disaster prediction, prevention, and relief).

Social studies education has several purposes. Narrowly constructed, it is the subject field that transmits socially approved ideas about citizenship.[14] However, Nelson shows the intellectual restrictions that accompany that limited purpose and argues that social studies educators must also mentor students in social inquiry through which they develop and use critical thinking skills used in reasoned decision making. This process may test accepted beliefs and students should be encouraged to do so. In the same vein, this Bulletin proposes that teachers engage in social inquiry and critical analysis of the complexities of the interaction of natural disasters and human rights.

Decision-making and social action skills are core elements of an effective citizenry. In Chapter 15, Previte explains how issues-centered education enriches the development of citizens in what Vinson describes as "informed social criticism."[15] And in Chapter 10, Pang examines the work of Nobel Peace Prize Laureate Muhammad Yunus and how he created an egalitarian organization, the Grameen Bank, which has empowered millions of women in a country that has experienced continual drought. The women have become owners of the Grameen Bank, building futures for themselves and their families. His work is an excellent subject for student-to-student human rights discussions.

One of the major goals of this Bulletin is to encourage social studies educators at all levels to incorporate scientific knowledge of natural disasters, in addition to examining issues that arise out of the conditions and problems that often accompany them. Elementary and secondary school students around the country are often involved in projects that benefit natural disaster victims, and they are engaged in deep discussions about the controversies surrounding disasters and relief efforts. Students must be encouraged to think beyond our national borders; both young and older

learners can start with discussion of natural disasters they have seen in their own communities or personal experiences. These may include the wildfires of California, floodwaters in North Dakota, or hurricanes or tornadoes in various states. Connecting the personal experiences of students with individuals around the world will provide an initial foundation for discussion. In Chapter 14, Pang and Oser give suggestions for teachers to guide younger learners in thinking about and involvement in social action in their communities first, and then nationally and internationally. In Chapter 16, Fernekes provides resources that can extend an educator's understanding of human rights and natural disasters.

Natural disasters continue to recur throughout the earth, making them a critical and timely topic for the social studies classroom. We believe that civic responsibility extends beyond students' schools or their local communities. We hope that this Bulletin on natural disasters will enable teachers to empower learners by investigating their interdependence with individuals and nations from around the world, while actively educating them to support and protect universal human rights.

NOTES

1. William F. Ruddiman, *Plows, Plagues & Petroleum: How Humans Took Control of Climate* (Princeton, NJ: Princeton University Press, 2005), 190.

2. Beverly Edmonds and William Fernekes, *Children's Rights: A Reference Handbook* (Santa Barbara, CA: AB-CLIO, 1996); Valerie Pang and Li-Rong Lilly Cheng. *Struggling to be Heard: The Unmet Needs of Asian Pacific American Children* (Albany, NY: SUNY Press, 1998).

3. Angus Gunn, *Encyclopedia of Disasters: Environmental Catastrophes and Human Tragedies, Vol. 1* (Westport, CT: Greenwood Press, 2008), xxiii.

4. *Ibid.*

5. This quotation is taken from Micheline R. Ishay's work, *The History of Human Rights: From Ancient Times to the Globalization Era* (Berkeley: University of California Press, 2004):3.

6. This quotation is taken from p. 1 of David Weissbrodt's "Human Rights: An Historical Perspective," in *Human Rights*, ed. Peter Davies (London: Routledge, 1988) 1-20.

7. Jack Donnelly, *Universal Human Rights in Theory and Practice*, 2d ed. (Ithaca: Cornell University Press, 2003), 1.

8. *Ibid.* 15.

9. Simon Romero, "With Haitian Schools in Ruins, Children in Limbo." *New York Times*, March 7, 2010, p. 6. Available at www.nytimes.com/2010/03/07/world/americas/07schools.html.

10. United Nations Human Development Programme, *Human Rights and Human Development* (New York: United Nations, 2000).

11. Willard Kniep, "Defining a Global Education By Its Content," *Social Education 50, 1986:437-446.*

12. Felisa Tibbitts and William R. Fernekes, "Human Rights Education" in *Teaching About Social Issues: Major Programs and Approaches*, ed. Samuel Totten and Jon Pedersen (Charlotte, NC: Information Age Publishing, 2010): 87-118.

13. Dennis N. Banks, "What is the State of Human Rights Education in K-12 Schools in the United States in 2000? A Preliminary Look at the National

Survey of Human Rights Education" (paper presented at the annual meeting of the American Educational Research Association, Seattle, Wa., April 2001) ERIC Document ED 454: 134.

14. Jack. L. Nelson, "Communities, Local to National, as Influences on Social Studies Education" in *Handbook of Research on Social Studies Teaching and Learning*, ed. James Shaver (New York: Macmillan, 1991): 332-341.

15. Kevin Vinson, " The 'Traditions' Revisited: Instructional Approach and High School Social Studies Teachers," *Theory and Research in Social Education 26* (1998): 50-82.

CHAPTER 2

DISASTERS: PAST, PRESENT, AND FUTURE

ANGUS M. GUNN

ABOUT 75,000 YEARS AGO, an Indonesian mountain known as Toba exploded into a massive eruption that changed the whole course of human history. The circumstances surrounding and following this event were so much more significant than any other known volcanic eruption that it became a worst-case model for geologists. Fortunately, nothing of comparable size has happened in the period of recorded human history. However, as we consider the interactions of disasters and humans, Toba is a valuable reference point. It is a reminder that disasters of this magnitude are possible. This was an eruption that carried into the atmosphere three thousand times the amount of rocks and ash that came from Mount St. Helens in 1980.[1]

The coincidence of Toba's explosion and the final phase of the great ice age, the Wisconsin, transformed human life more powerfully than any other known event within the past 100,000 years. Geological research in modern times uncovered evidence of this massive volcanic eruption. As the material from the eruption circled the earth, it blocked out the sun's rays all over the world for six years, lowering the already low temperature caused by the ice to -44°F/-42°C. Global temperatures stayed at a very low level for a further thousand years. During this period of time, drought and famine were widespread. Many of the larger forms of life, including large numbers of humans, died or were endangered.

This was the first volcanic eruption to threaten the whole human race. Fewer than thirty thousand humans survived by moving to warmer climates in Southern Africa. Rapid evolutionary changes occurred among them, as can happen in very small populations. In time, as climatic conditions improved, this remnant of humanity spread out across the whole world to form the human population of today. To test the validity of their calculations, geneticists examined the mitochondrial DNA of chimpanzees, our closest relatives in evolutionary terms, to find out if they, too, had been victims of the same environmental disaster. The results were conclusive. They had experienced an extreme reduction in numbers similar to the human one.

Defining Disasters: Does Natural Include Humans?

The word *disaster* has as many meanings as there are individuals who experience personal tragedies. For the person who loses a family member in a car accident, the event is certainly a disaster, and it is rightly so called. In this chapter, the definition follows the pattern used by most writers—a calamitous event occurring at one point in time and causing extensive destruction for many. Such events are called *natural* by some people (for example, hurricanes, cyclones, tsunamis, earthquakes, floods, volcanic eruptions, or pandemics) and other events are considered to be *human* if they involve terrorism, fires, chemical explosions, conflicts, oil spills, and the sinking of ships. In our contemporary world, the distinction between these two categories is disappearing as human action again and again appears to be the main causal factor in disasters, even in those that are floods or windstorms. When Hurricane Katrina struck New Orleans in 2005, many people saw it as a natural disaster. Most of the destruction, however, was caused by the failure of the levees. They had not been maintained at proper strength, and the city was flooded.

In Earlier Times

For most of recorded human history, it was not possible to prevent or minimize destruction caused by events like earthquakes, floods, or pandemics that were nonhuman disasters, because the levels of technology, understanding of tsunamis, and abilities to prevent river flooding were not sufficiently advanced.[2] Not until the second half of the nineteenth century did leaders in developing countries learn to anticipate and minimize the dangers from river flooding. China's Yellow River flood of 1887, the worst in the country's history, caused a death toll of 900,000 people. It could have been prevented if leaders had known more about the accumulation of soil in the bed of a river. Periodical removal of this soil would have been a better solution than trying to solve the problem by raising the mud levees higher and higher over time. The much smaller 1889 flood in Johnstown, Pennsylvania, also the worst in a nation's history, could have been prevented had more attention been paid to the sluiceways that maintained the height of water in the lake at a safe level.

The huge fire of 1871 that engulfed Chicago was preventable, had enough attention been given to what was known about fires and had adequate planning been made for dealing with the conflagration that broke out. Wood was the universal raw material for both buildings and streets at that time, and the authorities of a city with "windy" as part of its nickname should have been alert and prepared for any and every fire. Firemen were not told about the 1871 fire for an hour after it broke out, and they were then sent to the wrong location for a time, giving enough opportunity for the flames to expand out of control. In earlier centuries, as cities emerged, fires were treated as a part of life for which no provision was made to cope. They could be ignited by lightning or by human activity and then allowed to burn out, as was seen throughout the ages in cities as far apart in time as Rome, Italy, and London, England.

If we look farther back in time, there have been many different explanations for disasters that have made them appear to be beyond human control. One common explanation has been divine anger. Imagine the minds of people when, on November 1 (All Saints Day), 1755, Lisbon, Portugal, was hit with an earthquake of maximum power, followed by a series of tsunami waves that triggered fires all over the place. Almost everyone was in a church. The bewilderment was terrifying. More than 30,000 lost their lives, and destruction of the city's buildings was almost universal. Most people were convinced that all of this was a punishment from God because of their sins. If we go father back in time, to 1600, to the huge volcanic eruption that totally destroyed the city of Arequipa, Peru, and its surroundings, the role of theism is even more pronounced. A thousand people were killed. The Catholic priests had told the people, as small earthquakes gave warning of an approaching eruption, that there was going to be a terrible volcanic eruption from God to punish them for their sins.

In Modern Times

This long-standing interpretation of disasters of all kinds that persisted for more than a thousand years did not vanish immediately as scientific discoveries and fresh thinking replaced the old superstitions. Sudden changes in the normal patterns that prevailed over time continued to be regarded in some places as evidence of the actions of a higher power. Today, advances in technology and science give us both an understanding of the causes of the disasters that bewildered our forebears and provide clues on how to minimize their destructiveness. There are, however, negatives. Chemical industries worldwide cause havoc

in our air and water, greatly endangering our health. Technology raises individual behaviors to a new level of concern—a single error by one operator in a major chemical factory can kill thousands of people.

In 1976, at a chemical plant that manufactured herbicides in Seveso, Italy, one operator failed to switch on the cooling system. Dioxin, one of the most poisonous substances known, was released into the surrounding community with terrible consequences. In 1986, at the nuclear installation Chernobyl in the Ukraine of the old Soviet Union, one person failed to switch on the cooling water that would have prevented overheating of the reactor, causing the world's worst nuclear accident and flooding a whole continent with deadly radiation. Two years later, in India at Bhopal, a worker failed to turn on the warning siren when a leak of poisonous gas occurred. Eight thousand people were killed and another 250,000 seriously injured. A terrorist can blackmail a whole city, even a large part of a nation; one man did so in the U.S. in 2001 by spreading anthrax through the mail. Relationships and the social life of humans are now key elements of our environment because they may be the key to avoiding errant individual behavior.

Evidence of human involvement in what were regarded as purely natural disasters appeared increasingly in the early years of the twentieth century, beginning with the great San Francisco earthquake of 1906. In that earthquake, the accompanying firestorm did most of the destruction, not the shaking from the quake. Destruction could have been greatly minimized had an adequate fire prevention system been in place. After 1906, places that are in earthquake-risk areas gave new priority to fire prevention. Another feature of the San Francisco disaster became a model for other places in the proper use of fill land, underwater areas that were reclaimed and used as sites for homes. The fill land of the city, the Marina area, was severely damaged by the quake through liquefaction—the shaking of the relatively loose particles of soil and sand until they attracted water, turning what was solid land into a liquid into which buildings sank and collapsed. Fill lands were not suitable for multi-storey structures and recommendations were so made for the future guidance of the city managers.

This recommendation became a principle more frequently observed in the breach. Real estate development, right in the middle of a big city, was too much of a temptation for city officials. Whether as a result of bribery or something else, city after city throughout the world failed to follow the 1906 recommendations, with tragic results. Three are noted here. The strongest earthquake since the 1906 one struck the Santa

Cruz Mountains and the city of San Francisco in 1989. City authorities over the years had ignored the recommendations from 1906. They rebuilt the Marina fill area to use it as a site for the 1912 Panama-Pacific International Exhibition. When the 1989 quake struck, thousands of buildings were destroyed and sixty-three lives were lost. The area that suffered most damage was the Marina. Since 1989, the heights of buildings in this part of San Francisco are lower than formerly and part of the area is a park.

The stories in two other countries were similar to those of San Francisco. In the city of Brisbane, Australia, an over-70-year-old government regulation preventing any construction of buildings below a given elevation (based on earlier experiences of floods) was ignored, as had happened elsewhere. In 1974, the worst flood of the century swept over Brisbane. Everything on the prohibited lands was destroyed, and many lives were lost. Another example of the same tragedy occurred in Japan, in the city of Kobe, in 1995. For decades, this fast-growing center of Japanese industry and commerce had been reclaiming land from the sea and using the new areas for warehouses and shipping facilities. All of this work began long after 1906. When the earthquake struck, there was widespread liquefaction throughout the reclaimed areas. Warehouses and other installations sank and disintegrated, all roads and other communications disappeared, and the ground level dropped in elevation by several feet.

Cities and Disasters

Regarding the understanding and minimizing of the effects of disasters, the biggest series of changes in modern society was the emergence of big cities. Small cities have a long history, but the kind of multi-million-person urban areas of today are fairly new, dating for the most part from the 1950s. It was then that the improvement of medical services worldwide caused a dramatic cut in deaths, while birth rates remained high. Technological developments, at the same time, reduced labor demands in rural areas, and the migration to cities began and accelerated everywhere, somewhat like the race to cities in Britain a century earlier at the beginning of the Industrial Revolution. New York, in 1950, was the first city to have ten million people. By 1970, there were three cities with populations of more than ten million each, and by 1990 there were ten of these mega-cities. Any disaster in one of these places, whatever the cause, would inevitably be a costly and deadly tragedy. Today the world's ten biggest mega-cities are all populated at well over ten million, and three of them—Tokyo (29 million), Mexico City (18 million), and Jakarta (17 million)—are located in high-risk earthquake zones.

Even in cities much smaller than these, the high concentrations of people and buildings can lead to devastating costs when an earthquake strikes. Destruction is greatly increased when a disaster strikes a big urban center, not only on account of the damage done to the city, but also because of the harm done to the thousands of interdependent connections that tie the city to the rest of the world. In 1980, Miami-Dade County, home to more than two million people, experienced the most destructive hurricane of the twentieth century. More than $26 billion in costs was incurred to replace what was lost. Billions more were spent on the hundreds of thousands who had to be taken to sheltered locations. Nothing approaching this level of costs from a hurricane had ever been known before this time. It was a wake-up call to the nation. Imagine the global dislocation if a hurricane of this strength were to hit New York.

There are large gaps in the history of disasters because the details of many events that in all likelihood happened were never recorded anywhere. Geological research is unearthing many of these lost records and is also discovering recurrent rates for volcanic eruptions and earthquakes, that is to say, estimates of the times between events. For example, we now know the approximate dates for past eruptions of the Yellowstone Volcano. The last one was over 600,000 years ago. Because of the great time periods involved and the few past records available, it is impossible to predict when the next one will come. Nevertheless, one scientist pointed out that if the last one occurred 600,000 years ago, then it is possible that another similar one might come in this century. A different finding from geological research discovered a lot about a very powerful earthquake that struck Seattle in January of the year 1700, long before any westerners had reached this area. The exact date of the event is known from Japanese records because that country had experienced and recorded the date of an enormous tsunami that traveled across the Pacific at that time.

In the Future

In the year 2006, the world's longest running international science journal published the findings of a conference on world disasters and the future. This conference brought together scientists from all over the world, each one of whom specialized in one scientific aspect of the subject. The scientific aspect was stressed to make it clear that science is limited with regard to disasters. Many other institutions and competences are always needed. The phrase "Extreme Natural Hazards," rather than "disasters," was used to identify the subject matter of the conference.[3] The interesting aspect from this conference is how it came to be organized. The

Instructional and Classroom Applications

In every experience of disasters, local authorities have to deal with two things: (1) theft by irresponsible people who take advantage of the temporary disorder; (2) examination of ways to prevent recurrence of any aspects of a disaster.

When the German Zeppelin *Hindenburg* caught fire in New Jersey in 1937, some local people attempted to steal what they could of the cargo. The police made every attempt to arrest the thieves. In Lisbon, Portugal, in 1755, when a tsunami destroyed most of the city, the local authorities instructed police to shoot anyone they found stealing. What rules should be put in place today to cope with the danger of thievery in future disasters?

More and more in today's society, there are disasters due to human failure in the operation or maintenance of complex chemical installations. Many of these disasters are caused by operational changes that were made by management but not adequately explained to workers. The dioxin spill in Seveso, Italy, in 1976, happened as a result of a design change that was not explained fully to workers, with the result that they operated on one occasion on the basis of the former design. In 1988, in Bhopal, India, the management of the chemical company decided to use inexperienced workers because it was losing money by employing fully qualified ones. The results were devastating. If you were employed by the U.S. Government and responsible for approving new chemical manufacturing plants, how would you make sure that accidents such as the Seveso and Bhopal ones never happened again?

Japan is a densely populated country with limited amounts of flat land. Kobe is one of Japan's biggest industrial cities, with trade links to most of the world. It is a seaport, so, over the years, it reclaimed land from the sea to provide places for ships and storage buildings for the goods that the country exports and imports. During a major earthquake in 1995, most of these reclaimed lands were destroyed by liquefaction. Japan should have known about the danger of liquefaction because it had been informed of similar failures in other countries. What, in your opinion, should have been done by Kobe's leaders to make sure that its reclaimed land was not destroyed in 1995?

Royal Society took note of two extraordinary events in 2005 and one at the very end of 2004—the Indonesian Tsunami, the Katrina Hurricane, and the Pakistani earthquake. Scientists who had studied these disasters felt that they represented tragedies of such importance and significance that they carried implications for the immediate and more distant future.

The tsunami on December 26, 2004, was literally an earth-shattering one, without an equal in recorded history. The earth's rotation was slowed down by a small fraction of a second because of it. The earthquake that caused it was similar on the Moment Magnitude Scale (Mw=9-9.3) to those that struck Chile in 1960 (Mw=9.5) and Alaska in 1964 (Mw=9.2). No one in the U.S. Northwest will fail to take note of these connections when they think about the future. Throughout geological history, all around the Pacific in the so-called "ring of fire," there have been many earthquakes like these, and it is only within the last ten years that scientific journals have published firm evidence for a Mw=9.2 earthquake in and around Seattle in January of 1700. Furthermore, research into the frequencies of occurrence of an earthquake of this size in this same location revealed that they occur approximately every 300 years, so a repetition could come within the present century.

Another consideration arises from this terrible tsunami that swept across two continents, destroying property, coastal lands, and killing a quarter of a million people. If geologists can tell with such accuracy when Seattle was hit with a powerful earthquake and when it might be struck again, can they not also predict the likelihood of another tsunami like this one in 2004? The answer is: "Not yet." Many geologists who specialize in trends among past earthquakes and tsunamis have made some discoveries, but this branch of scientific research is still very young. Kerry Sieh of the California Institute of Technology is an expert in this field. He has already discovered a lot about the past history of the San Andreas fault in California, to the extent that he can make some predictions about the course of future earthquakes arising from it. In his work on Indonesian earthquakes, he is quite sure that one or two additional earthquakes and tsunamis that will be almost as powerful as the 2004 one will strike the coast of Sumatra sometime before the year 2050. He cannot be more accurate than this at the present time.

However, Sieh has extensively described what can be done to minimize destruction from tsunamis. He argues that most of the loss of life and damage to property in 2004 could have been avoided had there been emergency response preparedness of the kind with which we are familiar in the Western World.

The nations that were affected by the December 26 tsunami are, for the most part, developing countries. They do not have the national wealth to pay for installations of this kind. One of the first things done by all the countries affected by the disaster was to establish an organization to set up just such a warning system because now, in the light of the harm that was done, many countries from around the world helped with the cost of a warning system. When the tragedy of Pakistan's earthquake of 2005 is also reconsidered in the light of Indonesia's inadequate preparedness, the same reality applies. Like many of the developing Asian nations, Pakistan is a developing country that could have been greatly helped, and its death toll much reduced, had there been an emergency warning system in place.

Hurricane Katrina, the third of the dramatic events of late 2004 and 2005, points to the future in different ways, reminding us of the interlocking nature, what we sometimes call the global village, of all human activities. "No man is an island," said the poet John Donne, and now we know it. Katrina was the costliest and one of the deadliest hurricanes in the entire history of the U.S., yet the advance warnings from the National Weather Service could not have been better. With hindsight, it has to be said that this tragedy should never have happened. There are three lessons for the future that arise from it:

1. Carelessness in preparation, when there is warning of a major tragedy, has global repercussions. Oil prices worldwide increased because of the important role played by the Gulf and the processing sites around New Orleans. The U.S. trade deficit with Saudi Arabia increased by $40 billion.
2. U.S. infrastructure inadequacies, now widely recognized and demanding attention, caused failure of the New Orleans levees with disastrous consequences.
3. Global warming and climate change will increase the intensity and potential destruction of all future storms.

As we consider the future, a new word appears in the descriptions of disasters among scientific organizations. That word is *extreme*, and it points to increases in intensity and destructiveness in the years to come. Larger numbers of people, and human preferences for living in dangerous places, are two of the factors that contribute to this probability. As we reflect on all that has happened in the course of human history, giving consideration to successes as well as failures, we see humans coping better as they make use of advances in technology. Thus, we may be better prepared now than ever before for the extremes of the future. 🔰

NOTES

1. John Savino and Marie D. Jones, *Supervolcano: The Catastrophic Event that Changed the Course of Human History* (Franklin Lakes, NJ: New Page Books, 2007). This book deals with super volcanoes in general and Toba in detail, together with notes on the persistence of old theistic views on the causes of disasters.

2. Angus M. Gunn, *Encyclopedia of Disasters: Environmental Catastrophes and Human Tragedies*, 2 vols. (Westport, CT: Greenwood Press, 2008). Additional details on these and other modern disasters that are mentioned in this chapter can be found in these publications.

3. J.M.T. Thompson, Editor, *Philosophical Transactions of the Royal Society: Extreme Natural Hazards, volume 364, number 1845* (London, UK: The Royal Society, 2006). This collection of papers is an eye-opener on the variety and destructive power of possible future disasters.

CHAPTER 3

A GEOGRAPHIC PERSPECTIVE ON NATURAL DISASTERS

BILL PISARRA

GEOGRAPHY IS THE ANTITHESIS OF *SEINFELD*. *Seinfeld* was the TV show about nothing; geography is a discipline that includes everything. The geographic lens can have a wide focus (for example, the insatiable desire of Americans to consume shrimp at chain restaurants can be tied to the incredible toll the 2004 tsunami had on the small fishing villages of India); or it can be narrow, as is the case with the choices a few families make in deciding whether or not to rebuild in the floodplain after a flood destroys their homes.

Geography is the study of anything that varies over the surface of the earth, and geographers attempt to discern spatial patterns and identify the forces that interact to create or modify these patterns. Students are often introduced to the discipline through the study of five themes: location, place, region, movement, and human-environment interaction.[1] Of these, movement and human-environmental interaction are of special value in a geographic perspective on disasters and human rights.

Movement encompasses the study of shifts of physical items (e.g., tectonic plates or manufactured goods), people (e.g., migrations) and ideas (e.g., fashion or religion). Geographers attempt to understand why some things move and others don't. They examine patterns of diffusion, such as those that are contagious (e. g., the way a cold spreads) or those that are hierarchical (e.g., spreading through a hierarchy, an example being the way in which new French fashions first jump to Rome, then New York, and finally Tokyo). A general assumption is that the volume of movement will decrease over distance (distance decay), but contrary symptoms are particularly intriguing.

The movement of people is of special geographic interest. At the simplest level are factors that "push" people away from one place and/or "pull" them towards another. This concept is useful when applied to both natural disasters and human rights. One would expect that individuals would be pushed away from areas where they could be hurt by natural disasters and pulled towards safer areas. The history of natural disasters, however, demonstrates that this is not the case. These contrary symptoms stimulate geographers to search for reasons. This is a particularly compelling line of inquiry when natural disasters and human rights are examined in tandem. A simple analysis suggests that those with the fewest rights have very limited means and opportunities to move away from dangerous places for areas of greater safety and opportunity; distance decay does not seem to account for this.

Movement: Building on Floodplains

One key to a geographic perspective on natural disasters is understanding how people make decisions that move them into harm's way or in response to harm. Peter Haggett, in *Geography: A Global Synthesis*, reports on the work of geographers Gilbert White and Ian Burton.[2] White and Burton wanted to understand how individuals could make decisions regarding locations of residences and other structures that would, with some degree of certainty, put them at risk for being flooded. Such knowledge can contribute to public policy development that can limit future loss of life and property damage. White and Burton studied 498 U.S. urban communities that were subject to flooding. They examined how the frequency and severity of floods influenced attitudes towards flooding. They reported that residents of a place like Darlington, Wisconsin (which experiences floods about twenty times in any ten-year period) adopt an attitude of "optimistic rationalization" to justify their continued occupation of the floodplain. Haggett summarizes that in places where natural hazards occur at irregular intervals, people cope with the uncertainty by denial or faith:

- ▶ Eliminate the hazard by denial
  - ▶ Deny its existence: "It can't happen here"
  - ▶ Deny its recurrence: "It can't strike twice in the same place"
- ▶ Eliminate the irregularity by faith
  - ▶ Learn the frequency: "Floods come every five years"
  - ▶ Transfer responsibility to a higher power: "It's in the hands of God (or the government)"

Despite optimistic rationalization, disasters do strike, and they take a greater toll on marginal members of society who have the least control over where and how they live. When natural disasters strike rural populations, the poor, the sick, and the disenfranchised usually have few options for restoring their way of life. The marginalized are often forced to migrate, and without options to rebuild, they often abandon their rural life and means of support and migrate to urban centers. Here they live in slums in areas that the better off choose not to live in. Not only have the poor lost their livelihood and homes, their new living sites may be low-lying areas that expose residents to flood, chemicals, waterborne diseases, and diseases carried by swamp-dwelling animals, insects, and human waste.[3] The poor may live in structures that are situated on steep slopes susceptible to severe damage from earthquakes, hurricanes, and mudslides. In the event of disaster, these locations may be impossible for rescue and medical personnel to reach.

Examination of the movement of people (including both those by force or by choice), reasons for the movement, and the types of places to which movers relocate, offers a geographic dimension on natural disasters and their impact on human population and rights.

Human-Environment Interaction

The interplay between humans and the environment is another major geographic theme. At the beginning of the twentieth century, many geographers theorized that the environment dictated the actions of man. These environmental determinists became apologists for the second age of imperialism. By the mid-twentieth century, the environmental determinists had been discredited, and a new school of thought began to take shape. H. J. de Blij summarized this view succinctly: "Geographers study the reciprocal relationship between humans and environments."[4] This perspective yields a view that the environment has a significant and direct role in the activities of humans (e.g., we don't attempt to grow crops outdoors at the North Pole), as well as the view that humans have a profound impact on the environment.[5] Determinism can stunt inquiry, while the vitality of interaction offers significant opportunities for critical thinking and problem solving.

Long before humans arrived on the scene, hurricanes developed and remade islands and coast lines, volcanoes erupted and created mountains, ice sheets developed and receded to create valleys and rivers, plates slipped and pushed up mountains, and fires raged through forests and prairies. These events produced multiple environmental niches (e.g., forests, prairies, tundra, and deserts) required by many of earth's creatures, while affecting others more negatively.

As humans evolved and populations expanded, increasingly powerful technologies developed, giving people the ability to alter their environment. In relatively small and nomadic communities the impact of human activities on the environment was felt primarily at a local scale. Today that impact is felt on a global scale. The result is a greater risk from disasters, more frequent and more dangerous to more people. For example, an increase in both frequency and severity of hurricanes and typhoons seems tied to global warming—a development linked to humans.[6]

Where once floods were viewed as a gift of the gods, spreading the fertile silt that rivers carry across agricultural lands that were central to the development of great civilizations like Egypt, floods are now universally seen as disasters that require intervention and control. Most attempts at flood control result in fewer floods, but those that do occur are far more destructive. Alteration of existing space can lead to unintended consequences. Not only do attempts at flood control through dams, channel construction, and levee building increase the possibility of catastrophic floods, they fundamentally change the ecology of rivers. For example, levees prevent river sediment from being distributed across the floodplain. Sediment is then deposited in the main channel. Over time, the sediment in the main channel builds up, and the level of the levees must be raised. Fortunately, people have the capacity to undo some of the damage done. Recent experiments with dam removals have restored free-flowing rivers and environments suitable for aquatic insects and the fish that feed upon them.[7]

The theme of human-environmental interaction is illustrated in Galveston, Texas. In 1900, Galveston was a major port on the Gulf Coast, until it was struck by a fierce hurricane. Residents, either as the result of hubris or tenacity, were determined to rebuild. They even raised the island by 8 feet in an attempt to prevent severe damage from future hurricanes. To some degree, Galveston weathered a number of major hurricanes throughout the twentieth century. Then Hurricane Ike hit in 2008, virtually wiping out a number of Galveston coastal communities.[8] Instead of recognizing the futility involved, many of these communities have rebuilt or are in the process of rebuilding in the same locations.

Case Study: The Indian Ocean Tsunami

The geographic themes of movement and human-environmental interaction can be applied to the study of a recent event that is infrequently examined in social studies—shrimp farming and the 2004 Indian Ocean Tsunami.

Natural disasters can destroy lives and livelihoods in minutes, or they can strangle the life out of communities over months and years. Both fast-hitting and slow-acting natural disasters play out in the coastal fishing villages of India, the result of globalization (the creation of a global economy in which goods and capital flow in an almost frictionless state that is aided by technology) and an insatiable demand for shrimp in world markets. In the process of meeting this demand, the fundamental human rights of the residents of these communities, particularly those listed, are abrogated. While this case study focuses on the Indian Ocean Tsunami of 2004, the processes observed in these villages are evident worldwide, especially in mid-latitude coastal communities, and the geographic perspective facilitates examination of the issues on both micro and global levels.

Grescoe's *Bottomfeeder: How to Eat Ethically in a World of Vanishing Seafood*[9] makes some very important points:

> The Indian Ocean tsunami, the most destructive in human history, disrupted shipping lanes, altered coast lines, exposed ancient submerged temples, and left three hundred thousand people dead. Strangely, however, it may have been a minor incident compared to a slow-motion catastrophe that has been unfurling on the shorelines and creeks of Asia for the last two decades. Largely unnoticed in the West and abetted by the collusion of trade organizations, loan-granting banks, and foreign-exchange-hungry politicians, it is a disaster that is the undoing of the lives and livelihoods of tens of millions of coastal villagers—among the most powerless and voiceless members of societies—in the name of ever-cheaper protein and all-you-can-eat meal deals.[10]

Shrimp is one of the most prized proteins. With new and efficient means of transportation making it possible for agricultural products to be shipped profitably worldwide, shrimp farming has become a huge international business. The result has been much lower shrimp prices in the U.S.[11] for farmed shrimp (and a resultant increase in demand), which has produced human tragedy, severe environmental degradation, and an increase in the damage done by hurricanes and tsunamis.

Many shrimp farming ventures are located in coastal communities in tropical latitudes. Shrimp farms have been carved from creeks and mangrove swamps that have served these communities as breeding grounds for an enormous number of aquatic animals and have provided significant protection from the storm surges generated by hurricanes and tsunamis. Both the nutritional needs and economic needs of these communities have been met by the environmental niches they have occupied.

In India, shrimp farms are created by bulldozing ponds out of these swamps. The dry ponds are treated with urea and superphosphorous. Both provide nutrients for the plankton that the shrimp will feed on. The ponds are then filled with brackish water. Diesel oil is pumped onto the surface to kill insect larvae. The water itself is treated with many chemicals to kill off any aquatic life that might compete with the shrimp. Throughout the six month growing cycle, the ponds are treated with pesticides, piscicides, and antibiotics. At the end of the cycle, the ponds are drained into the creeks, and the shrimp harvested. The chemical stew in which they have been reared is released into the environment.[12] This cycle is repeated over and over again. The first to feel the impact of the production process are the workers who often become sick from the chemicals to which they are exposed.[13]

Beyond the personal health considerations in this cycle, there are economic, social, and political repercussions, including human rights issues. Because some of the shrimp farms are created from converted rice paddies, jobs are lost. A one-acre rice paddy employed fourteen individuals. Only one person is needed for a one-acre shrimp pond. Moreover, the repeated release of chemicals into the creeks destroys much of the aquatic life that the local individuals had fished. Simultaneously, the same processes destroy the mangroves—further limiting the productive capacity of the environment and reducing the natural protection from hurricanes and tsunamis. When the 2004 tsunami hit those who lived in areas where there had been little or no loss of mangroves, villagers escaped with little or no loss of life. Where the mangroves had been destroyed, the loss of life was staggering. Indian aquaculture promoters attempted to use the 2004 tsunami as a way to further reduce the interference of local fisher people in the expansion of fish farms. The fisher people who had not already been driven to the cities in search of employment were now offered subsidized housing at inland locations that would have forced them to give up fishing.[14] It was the effective lobbying of the aquaculture interests that led to the creation of the subsidized housing programs.

In order to protect both the coastal environment and its inhabitants, in 1996, the Indian Supreme Court prohibited the

Instructional and Classroom Applications

Social Studies Standards
❸ PEOPLE, PLACES, AND ENVIRONMENTS
❾ GLOBAL CONNECTIONS

The geographic perspective can be best explored through case studies. Unfortunately, there are many recent examples of natural disasters (exacerbated by human action) in which human rights have been short changed.

Case studies may be pursued through a two-step process. First, students should be introduced to the Universal Declaration of Human Rights (UDHR). Students can then be provided with one or more articles describing both a natural disaster (e.g., Hurricane Katrina) and its impact on human populations. Students can work in groups to identify violations of the UDHR that they find in the articles. As groups present their cases, the instructor can follow up with questions that begin to expose causal chains.

Then, having demonstrated linkages between natural disasters and human rights, groups should be ready to find their own examples. Using either Internet resources or media center resources, groups should be encouraged to identify a specific example of a natural disaster (created or exacerbated by human action) in which human rights were abridged at a specific location. The teams should report on how man contributed to the disaster (human-environment interaction), which populations suffered the most and why (preferably through exploring causal linkages), which articles of the UDHR were violated, and policies that would help avoid both natural disasters and human rights abuses.

construction of new fish farms within a half-kilometer of the high tide mark.[15] The economically advantaged have found it relatively easy to bypass this law and continue to develop new farms. The beneficiaries of shrimp farming have avoided the new law simply by making sure the high-tide line is never demarcated. This boundary has great relevance for those who can no longer reap their fundamental needs from the water around them.[16]

India is not the only country to suffer the ill effects of shrimp farming. Grescoe cites one study that attributes 38% of mangrove losses worldwide to shrimp farming . He goes on to report that Ecuador has lost 70% of its mangroves to satisfy the demand of America's chain restaurants.[17]

Every step in this process illustrates human-environmental interaction. Both humans and the environment suffer from the interaction. Who benefits? Clearly, consumers from the developed world benefit from cheap shrimp (especially if you discount the potential health implications from eating shrimp grown in a chemical stew). The real beneficiaries are the huge agricultural conglomerates that provide the feed and chemicals used in aquaculture. As it turns out, the local shrimp farmers made out well in the early days. But there is so much competition today that the price to the producer has dropped significantly. As the local shrimp farmers attempt to eke out a small profit, they are forced to buy feed and chemicals from a handful of agribusiness conglomerates that dominate the world market—these huge agribusinesses are the big winners.[18]

Natural Disasters and Human Rights: Geographical Implications

Examining the lives of these coastal producers demonstrates that human rights abuses are likely outcomes of movement decisions and patterns of human-environment interaction that either cause or result from natural disasters. The farmer who loses his life because the mangroves that protected him from tsunamis were destroyed, lost his rights to life and security. When aquaculture interests prevent the demarcation of the high-tide line and block implementation of laws that will stop the spread of shrimp farms, the "will of the people" as the basis of governmental authority is thwarted. When people are engaged in a primary economic activity (e.g., hunting, fishing, mining, or farming) and the resource is effectively destroyed, their rights to work and choice of employment have been crushed. When their way of life has been destroyed and when friends and family have been killed as the result of manageable natural disasters (i.e., mangrove loss increases deaths), it is impossible to achieve "a standard of living adequate for the health and well being" for individuals or groups.

Woody Guthrie chronicled the rights abuses of the men, women, and children who fled the Dust Bowl in his album *Dust Bowl Ballads*. At the time, the concept of human rights was neither well known nor well defined. Not until the UN's founding did an international organization pursue the work of codifying universal human rights. The result was the development of the Universal Declaration of Human Rights (UDHR), adopted in 1948 by the UN General Assembly. Key articles of the UDHR can be used to judge the human rights impact of shrimp farming on marginal coastal populations, particularly following natural disasters. Among these are UDHR articles:

- ▶ ARTICLE 3—Everyone has the right to life, liberty and security of person.
- ▶ ARTICLE 21—The will of the people shall be the basis of authority of government.
- ▶ ARTICLE 23.1—Everyone has the right to work, to free choice of employment.
- ▶ ARTICLE 25—Everyone has the right to a standard of living adequate for the health and well being of himself and of his family, including food, clothing, housing and medical care.

Humans have developed the means to wreak disaster on the earth that would far exceed that of other known disasters, short of a collision with a huge asteroid. A nuclear war could transform our planet into a wasteland—the ultimate human disaster. This would also be the ultimate human rights violation, as well as environmental catastrophe; the acts of a tiny minority would destroy the lives of billions and alter life on earth.

When researchers delve into airplane accidents they often find that the accident resulted from a series of interconnected decisions (e.g., taking off without enough fuel) and circumstances (e.g., weather being worse than predicted). When natural disasters result in the significant loss of human life, the study of these events reveals similar interconnections. All too often, we find that the poor and marginalized suffer disproportionately to the general population. Study of these events ultimately must focus on what happened to a specific group of people in a specific place. The geographic perspective utilizes all of the subfields of geography (e.g., physical, medical, political, cultural, and religious) to analyze the multiple causal chåains that result in these tragedies.

The Indian Ocean Tsunami of 2004 impacted many lives. Application of the geographic perspective helps one understand both the obvious causes of this disaster as well as the deep and complex web of human and environmental processes affecting the daily lives of people worldwide. These same inquiry tools can be used to study why marginal populations are more at risk from natural disasters and subsequent abuses that occur during recovery, and how such risks can be minimized in the future.🔷

NOTES

1. H. J. DeBlij, Alexander B. Murphy and Erin H Fouberg, *Human Geography: People, Place, and Culture*, 8th ed. (Hoboken, New Jersey: John Wiley and Sons, 2007), 11.

2. Peter Haggett, *Geography: A Global Synthesis* (Harrow, England: Pearson Hall, 2001), 357.

3. Janet Abramovitz, "Unnatural Disasters—Worldwatch Paper 158," *World Watch Institute*, Worldwatch Paper 158 (October 2001): 7, can be accessed at: www.worldwatch.org/system/files/EWP158.pdf, (accessed August 27, 2009).

4. DeBlij, Murphy and Fouberg, 11.

5. William H. Thomas, ed., *Man's Role in Changing the Face of the Earth—Volumes I and II* (Chicago: University of Chicago Press, 1956).

6. Pew Center on Global Climate Change, "Hurricanes and Global Warming FAQs" (Arlington, Virginia, 2009), www.pewclimate.org/hurricanes.cfm#freq, (accessed August 10, 2009).

7. American Rivers, "The Ecology of Dam Removal: A Summary of Benefits and Impacts" (Washington, D.C., February 2002, www.americanrivers.org, 3), can be accessed at: www.michigandnr.com/PUBLICATIONS/PDFS/fishing/dams/EcologyOfDamRemoval.pdf, (accessed August 10, 2009).

8. *The Boston Globe*, "The short—but eventful—life of Ike" (Boston, Massachusetts, September 15, 2008), www.boston.com, can be accessed at: www.boston.com/bigpicture/2008/09/the_short_but_eventful_life_of.html, (accessed August 10, 2009).

9. Taras Grescoe, *Bottomfeeder: How to Eat Ethically in a World of Vanishing Seafood* (New York: Bloomsbury USA, 2008), 147-175.

10. Grescoe, 149.

11. In a 2004 article, the *Wall Street Journal* reported that wholesale shrimp prices in the U.S. fell approximately 40% between 1997 and 2002. www.eiu.edu/~dr-davis/resources/%20Shrimp%20Industry%20%20Fight%20Looms.pdf, (accessed July 28, 2009).

12. Grescoe, 158.

13. Nityanand Jayaraman, "Against All Odds: Communities Asserting Their Rights to Food—A Dalit Village's Fight Against Industrial Aquaculture," *Speak Out!* (June 2007), 1-12, can be found at www.foodsov.org/resources/againstallodds.pdf, p. 9, (accessed July 28, 2009).

14. Grescoe, 163.

15. Grescoe, 163.

16. The study of boundaries is an essential part of the examination of political geography.

17. Grescoe, 160.

18. Grescoe, 165.

CHAPTER 4

THE PSYCHOLOGICAL IMPACT OF NATURAL DISASTERS IN SCHOOL

MARC NORMAN

DISASTERS ARE ABNORMAL SITUATIONS involving normal people, and those affected by them demonstrate an enormous range of emotional expressions. Educators who are engaged in responding to natural disasters face many challenges. Educators are sources of emotional support for students, as well as sources of academic and social education, but they have limited resources to deal with the full range of students' emotions, even in the best of situations. Educators must invariably struggle with a lack of experience and training, and are confronted by the need to use strained resources in the context of a chaotic, ever-changing environment. The rules seem unclear and constantly change—this is the very nature of disasters.

This chapter will offer guidance to teachers on dealing with the psychological impact of natural disasters in educational settings. Natural disasters include weather-related events (ice and snow storms, tornadoes, and hurricanes), toxic exposures (chlorine leaks), fires, and earthquakes. In all the above-mentioned cases, the goal of disaster mental health intervention is to mitigate significant emotional long-term harm and maximize successful adaptation strategies.

The Role of the School

In times of disaster, schools may serve to shelter the displaced community. Schools are often ideal because their size allows for large gatherings. Physically, they may be able to accommodate those with special needs and physical disabilities. Schools have parking lots, cafeterias, bathrooms and shower facilities, and audio-visual capabilities; however, in the long-term, schools cannot be all things to all people. Gyms and classrooms must be converted back to a place of learning, individuals will have to find other accommodations, and routines will need to be restored. Less tangibly, but still importantly, schools provide familiarity, shared experiences, cohesion, and a sense of community ownership and pride.

As students look to their teachers for encouragement and stability, the community looks to schools to provide safety in chaos and turmoil, but challenges exist. Educators are suddenly thrust into unfamiliar circumstances and must often work in an unstable and unpredictable environment. They are forced into roles they were not trained for or experienced in. This role change may be unwelcome and be its own traumatic experience. In some cases, the media may portray the response in an unfavorable light, and the mere presence of media can be distressing. Suddenly external eyes can magnify preexisting challenges, and there may be misperceptions and misunderstandings that are clearer in hindsight. Most people are not familiar or comfortable with that level of scrutiny. A goal of disaster intervention is to provide stability and predictability as quickly as possible; however, no one can predict how long and to what extent the physical and emotional effects will last.

Natural Disasters and Resulting Emotional Effects

Disaster environments are complicated, and no two disasters are alike. Multiple factors affect how and to what degree people will be emotionally and behaviorally affected. In some scenarios, the extent of damage to or availability of the school may be limited or nonexistent. Detailed response plans may not work as personnel may not be available, and deaths or injuries related to the disaster add significant stress to the situation.

The interaction of multiple factors shapes how the immediate and long-term response occurs. Predicting how long a disaster will evolve or how great the impact will be can help the school prepare and plan for how the students and community will respond, and appropriate material and personnel resources can be considered. Planning for how long the school will be inaccessible will help reduce anxiety and fear of the unknown. At the individual and community levels, a "one-time" or unique disaster, such as a toxic chlorine exposure from an overturned vehicle (with no physical school damage), will have less long-term impact than an unpredictable, unforeseen earthquake causing structural damage. In some cases, recurrent events may desensitize intense feelings, but in other cases, the new event heightens emotions left from the last event.

Symbolism and triggers are important concepts in the development of post-traumatic distress. If a disaster occurs when school is in session, individuals will make sensory associations between the trauma, school, and individuals at the school. When the school returns to its schedule, students (and even staff) may want to avoid the sensory triggers that worsen negative symptoms. Even seemingly insignificant objects or their absence may convey a sense of anger, fear, or loss to an individual. An on-property event and the associated symbols can disrupt the educational process more than off-property events when school is not in session. As educators move toward rebuilding or recovery, they should consider the *shared meaning* of objects. A given object may bring negative emotions for some, but a sense of closure for others. The same object can hold opposite significance for different individuals. For example, the site of a building that collapsed, killing adults and children, may be a source of tension in a community. Some will want the building rebuilt as a sign of recovery and strength, while others will want the structure removed because its very presence reminds them of their loved one's death or injury. These types of schisms and disagreements about how to recover may undermine the collaborative process necessary for rebuilding.

Finally, the nature of community and individual exposure to a disaster influences the ways in which students and staff are affected. Disasters can either be evolving or one-time events. For example, a flood may rise and fall for days or weeks, or there may be aftershocks after an earthquake. These types of situations give the sense of an emotional rollercoaster with ups and downs; in contrast, a toxic leak may clear after a few hours. The psychological impact of these events is different because in the case of the former event, the community becomes fatigued after increased anxiety and poor sleep for an extended period of time. Another aspect of how people respond to the disaster is the degree to which the individual was exposed to the trauma. Those who were more directly exposed (witnessed a death or accident) commonly experience a greater psychological impact than those on the periphery (someone who was evacuated on the other side of campus). The immediate exposure is different, although both cases have a psychological impact. In these cases, a form of psychological triaging may help identify those who may be more vulnerable to significant emotional distress.

Disaster Experiences: Five Phases

Disasters and disaster response tend to be dynamic, evolving events. Zunin and Meyers conceptualize these phases as warning, rescue or heroic, honeymoon, disillusionment, and recovery and reconstruction.[1] The timing of these phases, whether or not they are present, and the extent to which they occur, are disaster specific. For example, some disasters do not have a warning phase. Models like this can help conceptualize how individuals and communities are progressing from the initial stages of a disaster into the long-term recovery, and common emotional responses may be anticipated.

Some natural disasters have a *warning* phase. In a hurricane, there may be days of warning and uncertainty prior to the hurricane that affect the lives of those preparing for disaster. The impending potential disaster is well known, and there may be time to react, enabling communities to avoid or mitigate the impact by moving out of the storm's predicted path or boarding up windows. The warning phase is characterized by increased anxiety, worry, and vulnerability, but these emotions wax and wane as new information comes, and frustration may occur as the storm changes and predictions prove inaccurate.

When the event arrives, emergency service workers and those within the immediate disaster zone switch to the *rescue/heroic* phase, and the duration depends on how the disaster evolves. In ongoing events, such as a rising and falling flood, there may be a week-long rescue/heroic phase, as compared to a toxic exposure, where a school may be evacuated for an hour. It is at this time that a sense of unification for a common cause happens. This "fight or flight" period may bring shock, initial grief, and disorientation.

The next phase, the *honeymoon*, is relatively shorter. People often think, "it could have been worse," and may feel grateful. There may be a sense of relief that the immediate danger is over, but this is generally short-lived.

In the next two stages, disillusionment as well as recovery and reconstruction, community emotions may be the most intense. *Disillusionment* brings elements of reality to the situation. Individuals and communities begin to consider how the situation (or the worst parts of it) could have been avoided, and anger and blaming may be directed at individuals or systems. These intense emotions can be exacerbated by emotional and physical fatigue.

In the final stage, *recovery and reconstruction*, communities begin rebuilding the physical and emotional damage. Physical recovery may not begin for months or even years, so frustration is common, as many impatiently want "everything to return to normal." In many cases, "normal" will never occur, as the reality of vulnerability and potential for a similar disaster occurring again is realized. Planning for this disappointment and negative reaction can be anticipated and mitigated.

Psychological Aspects of Disaster

Disasters are abnormal situations, so most negative reactions to disaster are not "abnormal" or "pathological." There is a large range of "normal" behavior, and it is important not to pathologize atypical behavior within a disaster setting. Nervousness, anxiety, and worry are common and manifest in different ways. Symptoms can be separated into emotional/affective, behavioral/physical, and cognitive manifestations (see Table 1). Education may reduce symptoms, often referred to as "normalizing." Most symptoms will resolve without intervention; however for a minority, the symptoms are highly distressing and affect daily functioning.

Adults and children react differently to stress, and children's reactions are largely influenced by their developmental level and the reactions of adults around them. Young children lack the verbal ability to express their distress and concern. Thus, their distress often manifests in behavioral changes (see Table 2). In school, they may have decreased school performance, regression of behaviors, or an increase in aggressive play, possibly with themes of the trauma. Some of this increased stress may be triggered by upheaval within the home or feelings of misperceived guilt. Later, they develop different cognitive models for dealing with trauma. They are more likely to express their distress through behavioral outbursts, physical complaints, and nightmares. Importantly, children react to adult's reactions. Adults may feel that they are masking and hiding the significance of a disaster, but children are often aware that "something is wrong." The amount of information they should have and the manner in which it is disseminated to them is dependent on their developmental level, which is discussed below. Children are often afraid because of the unknown. The "unsaid" distress may increase children's anxiety because they imagine the worst

Table 1. Emotional, Behavioral, and Cognitive Symptoms of Stress

Affective/Emotional	Behavioral/Physical	Cognitive
Depression	Chills	Re-visualizing experience
Agitation	Shaking/tremor	Intrusive thoughts
Panic	Shortness of breath	Reliving past trauma
Fear	Sweating	Confusion
Anger	Restlessness	Decreased attention/concentration
Shock	Change in sleep	Hypervigilance
Denial	Withdrawal	Uncertainty
Crying	Vomiting	
	Headache	
	Elevated blood pressure	
	Rapid heart rate	

Table 2. Children and Adolescent Reactions to Stress

Young Children (up to age 6)	Older Children (age 6-10)	Adolescence (age 11+)
A sense of helplessness	Preoccupied talking about the event	A sense that the world is less safe
Fear	Diminished concentration	High-risk behaviors
Irritability	Sadness	Social anxiety
Crying	Anger	Feelings of being overwhelmed
Need for attention	Fear of recurrence	
Seeking affection/Being clingy		

scenario, including even unrealistic or improbable outcomes.

Teachers, staff, and administrators are not immune to similar distress. While trying to help others, they are challenged with their own lives, families, and personal loss. But the overall system goal is to restore the sense of stability and predictability, even within a chaotic situation. In the short- and intermediate-terms, individuals may experience worsening trauma from cumulative stress (from earthquake aftershocks, etc.). In the long-term (even a year or more after a disaster), individuals and communities may still be "temporarily" relocated, and anniversaries may bring back memories causing retraumatization.

While some of the aforementioned symptoms are common during and after a disaster, greater concern is warranted for more intense, prolonged reactions. When numerous symptoms manifest and affect a person's life, a clinical disorder may be present. The severity and duration of symptoms vary considerably. The major activity of disaster mental health is to mitigate pathological reactions, but several clinical disorders may be identified in this context, as well as those with pre-existing clinical disorders. For example, clinical anxiety disorders may be triggered by a disaster and can be considered to be typical reactions in terms of severity and duration. Individuals who are affected may experience a reduction in awareness (as if being in a daze) and feel like things are not real or like they are viewing themselves from the outside. These symptoms last for a minimum of 2 days and a maximum of 4 weeks, and occur within 4 weeks of trauma. Where adults may experience intense fear, helplessness, or horror, children's distress may be manifested as disorganized or agitated behavior. Negative feelings are dealt with by avoiding places, activities, and conversations that may worsen anxiety.

Rebuilding and Resiliency

There are many challenges when working in a disaster environment, but the overall goal is to resume learning without extended delay. For this to happen, schools must minimize the impact of the disaster by providing a safe learning environment for students, teachers, and staff. Long-term consequences of prolonged stress for teachers and staff include burnout, manifesting as emotional detachment, loss of mental energy, cynicism, and negative attitudes toward one's self and others. Practically, there are many obstacles that make long-term care difficult. The community may find that some individuals want to recover and move on quickly, while others want more time to process the trauma. In these cases, administrators must be sensitive to these issues and support myriad concerns.

Even with all of these complexities, there are several general principles that educators may use when working with students in a natural disaster. Supportive, empathetic leadership is a critical piece of successful recovery and rebuilding. Perceived messages of "suck it up" or no response to the emotional concerns of teachers, staff, and students can increase distress and feelings of isolation and helplessness. Leaders must convey a sense of hope and positive expectations, while appearing honest and credible; however, being overly optimistic and sending overly encouraging messages lessens a leader's credibility.

While not the focus of this chapter, it is worthwhile to note that there are many models of disaster mental health intervention. Few models are specific to children; however, the Sanford Model was developed by Nancy Sanford (following the Oklahoma Murrah Federal Building bombing in 1995) for a school setting. A recent, comprehensive disaster intervention is described in the Psychological First Aid (PFA) manual.[2] This was developed by the National Child Traumatic Stress Network and National Center for PTSD[3] and has intervention models for children. This manual is evidence-informed, detailing basic standards that can be used in actual events. Importantly, the PFA manual discusses cultural influences. These resiliency intervention models are designed to be time-limited and focus on the immediate crisis.

The concept of resiliency is widely used in disaster and crisis intervention, from local disasters to military settings. The basic concept is that, on balance, people are resilient and have inherent coping mechanisms to deal with disaster. Resiliency posits that even though the situation may be novel, most people recover on their own by using their existing personal resources (their inner strength). This concept works on the idea that most reactions are normal, not pathologic, and people may be more willing than not to talk about "resiliency" than "emotional trauma," a term which has a negative connotation. Although most people will recover using resiliency, some individuals will require greater support.

Several groups are considered to be more vulnerable to the emotional effects of trauma. First, children and adults with preexisting emotional disturbances, or who were struggling with traumatic events prior to the disaster, are more likely to need greater mental health support. Another vulnerable group is students with intellectual challenges. Typically, these children have difficulty when losing their routines and being placed in novel situations. Students with emotional disturbances or cognitive challenges are often identified before the natural disaster so they can be considered early on for additional support and the rapid establishment of structure; however, some children have not been recognized prior to a disaster. Of these unidentified children, those who are absent more after than before the disaster, and whose absence is not explained by relocation, accessibility to the school, or extenuating circumstances (family member's death, injury, or illness), are of particular concern. School personnel may not see that they are struggling and in need of help. Follow-up calls to these children's parents may be useful in identifying and treating these children so they can resume learning in a supportive environment.

No matter what intervention model is used, educators can use general tips in disaster settings. At the administrative level, interventions need to be consistent and coordinated throughout the school and district. The staff should use consistent messages and language to facilitate understanding and a coherent, supportive message. A challenge in trying to provide a consistent message is to demonstrate sensitivity to diverse languages, races, ethnicity, traditions, and beliefs. Unintended slights may be perceived when these issues are not considered, and it may be difficult to provide quick, accurate information in a school with parents who speak many languages.

In addition to consideration of demographic factors, interventions need to be age appropriate. Young students have different needs, and the interventions need to be at their developmental level. For example, young children do not understand that death is permanent, but older children may be capable of understanding this. Whether young or old, children and staff need the opportunity to express their grief in their own way. Administrators can help with reassurance and confidence by dispelling rumors and myths, which are often counterproductive and may increase anxiety in a time of chaos. Setting a calm, direct, informative, authoritative, nurturing, and problem-solving oriented tone will help inspire the community, and modeling this behavior by supporting teachers and the staff can allay many fears and concerns.

Conclusion

The interactions of natural disasters and emotions is highly complex and difficult to appreciate during an event. It is difficult to prepare for the unknown, and the realities of a natural disaster are typically worse than planned for, since systems do not plan for emotional consequences. Understanding the significant long-term emotional effects may help educators better respond to student, school, and community needs. 🔊

NOTES

1. Leonard Zunin and Diane Meyers, *Training Manual for Human Service Workers in Major Disasters, 2nd Ed.* (Washington, DC: Department of Health and Human Services Substance Abuse and Mental Health Services Administration, Center for Mental Health Services, DHHS Publication No. ADM 90-538, 2000).

2. Josef I. Ruzek, Melissa J. Brymer, Anne K. Jacobs, Christopher M. Layne, Eric M. Vernberg, and Patricia J. Watson, "Psychological First Aid," *Journal of Mental Health Counseling*, 29, n. 1 (January 2007): 17-49.

3. Center for Mental Health Studies in Schools, (Retrieved on July 11, 2009), smhp.psych.ucla.edu.

CHAPTER 5

DISASTERS AS THREATS TO PEACE

JEFFREY W. HELSING

The Links between Natural Disasters and Violent Conflict

Natural disasters are threats to peace around the world. In order to understand the link between natural disasters and violent conflict, it is important to consider natural disasters more broadly. A natural disaster cannot be defined as a single cataclysmic event, but rather as the consequences of an event or events triggered by forces of nature that overwhelm local response capacity and seriously affect the social and economic development of a community or society.[1] Therefore, the link between natural disasters and conflict is fairly simple—natural disasters have the potential to promote intrastate conflict by increasing competition among groups for scarce resources (e.g., arable land, food, water, fuel, housing, medicine, and relief aid). Such scarcities, in turn, provoke frustrations, which lead to anger and violence.[2] The likelihood of such conflict emerging is much more likely in poorer, more undeveloped countries because prevailing conditions that are conducive to conflict already exist. In addition, disasters can present long-term structural challenges to affected states that extend beyond the more immediate dangers. "Natural disasters affect the structures of society by disrupting economic development, by increasing income and wealth inequality, by marginalizing certain groups, and by leading to large-scale migrations. Crucially, natural disasters can also weaken state capacity and legitimacy, creating opportunities for the disgruntled to engage in violent resistance."[3]

The relationship between natural disasters and conflict is threefold:

▶ A natural disaster will exacerbate a conflict that is already unfolding by increasing competition among groups for scarce resources;

▶ A natural disaster can create conditions of privation and stress on governmental and social institutions that can lead to increased violence and cleavages in communities; and

▶ When a natural disaster strikes in a society already engaged in violent conflict, it is very difficult to develop a meaningful response to meet the needs of the victims of the disaster.

There are two caveats to this relationship. First, there is little evidence that a natural disaster is the primary cause of a violent conflict; such disasters often exacerbate existing conditions with the result that violent conflict is made worse or more likely. Second, slow-onset disasters (desertification, famine) are much more likely to contribute to conflict than rapid-onset disasters (typhoon, earthquake, volcanic eruption), because disasters such as famine or drought that develop over time undermine long-term economic and social well-being and create conditions of competition between communal groups over scarce resources. The long-standing crisis in Darfur is an interesting example of this. Ongoing drought in the African Sahel intensified grievances in Sudan, particularly about land use, and generated conflict between farmers and herders in the Darfur region. As such conflicts escalated, particularly along identity lines, the government of Sudan began to use Arab tribal militias to suppress the political aspirations of rebel groups in Darfur (driven in part by a desire to gain greater control over land use in the territory).[4]

For most experts on international conflict and political science, natural disasters cannot be divorced from international relations or the politics of the disaster's locale. Natural disasters are not disconnected from the dynamics of the society in which the disaster strikes and will reflect whatever political, social, and economic realities exist there. The disaster may be believed to have occurred because of the "hand of God" or forces of nature, but the consequences and effects will certainly be determined in large measure by the political, economic, and social conditions and institutions of the victimized area. This is because the impact of a natural disaster is not just physical, geological, or geographic, but also affects the human condition. Politics affect not only how a country or society feels the impact of the disaster, but also affects the provision of aid to those victimized by the disaster.

How a Disaster Can Produce Civil Conflict

A disaster produces civil conflict by first creating conditions of environmental and social distress. Civil conflict is made more likely by a disaster and can spread beyond the immediate area or beyond borders, because natural disasters create resource scarcities and resource competition. Disasters also can produce civil conflict by creating conditions of environmental and social distress that often lead to a crisis of legitimacy for the governing regime, particularly if the disaster is severe or inadequately handled.[5] For example, in the area of Balakot in Pakistan, fundamentalist Muslim groups were able to provide immediate relief that was quicker and to a greater degree than that which the government could provide after a devastating earthquake in October 2005, which prompted fertile recruiting ground for pro-violence extremist groups from a population disillusioned and let down by its government.[6]

Forty years earlier, another earthquake devastated northwest Pakistan. At the time, Pakistan was in a tense border conflict with India. The Pakistani government's response was also inadequate, and there was weakened public support within Pakistan for the government. Interestingly, India did not use the occasion to put more pressure on Pakistan for concessions in the ongoing dispute, but Pakistan became confrontational within a few months to divert attention away from its poor performance during the natural disaster. Failure by the state to respond to the basic needs and provide basic services such as health, shelter, and other means of support for victims can erode the social contract between state and citizens, which, in many cases, can lead to increased political instability, and potentially violent conflict. In 1992, when a devastating earthquake hit Cairo, the Egyptian government's response was slow and inadequate. Confidence in the government eroded significantly, and greater support for more extreme political and religious groups rose because they were able to respond to the disaster in a more timely and confidence-building manner than had the Egyptian authorities. The Anastasio Somoza regime's poor response to the 1972 Nicaraguan earthquake is believed by many to have contributed to the victory of the Sandinista movement in overthrowing Somoza seven years later. The same can be said for the earthquake in Iran in 1978: the poor response weakened the already shaky authority of the Shah.

Consequences, not Causes

Most conflict analysts agree that there is no single cause of conflict. There are a number of deep-rooted background conditions and sources of conflict that make conflict more likely. These include circumstances that make societies more vulnerable, such as lack of resources, the pressures of overpopulation, economic weakness, and social cleavages based on identity. Ineffective governance and incompetent leadership, along with weak economic, social, and political institutions, all combine to make some countries more vulnerable to conflict than others. These factors are compounded when there is an imbalance of political and socio-economic opportunities among different identity groups and little or no active and organized civil society.

Countries that are burdened with such circumstances are much more likely to suffer from a natural disaster, and, for some, the natural disaster may become either an aggravating factor that makes violent conflict more likely, or the natural disaster may become the triggering event for violence, much like other triggering events such as an assassination, military coup, or collapse of a country's currency or economic institutions. There are a number of aggravating factors that contribute to a climate conducive to violent conflict: the widespread availability of weapons, widespread corruption and public waste, excessive capital outflows (sending money out of the country), significant displacement of populations, and deterioration of public services. With the exception of arms availability, natural disasters often exacerbate these aggravating factors, therefore enhancing the possibility of violent conflict resulting. Natural disasters are destabilizing—already weakened countries have a much more difficult time dealing with the resulting instabilities than those that have stronger economic, political, and social institutions. As an example, the Island of Hispaniola has faced many devastating storms and hurricanes, but the less stable country of Haiti (on the west side of the island) has been much more negatively affected by such disasters than the more stable Dominican Republic (on the east side of the island).

The consequences of natural disasters are often similar to the consequences of warfare. The effects of natural disasters are usually magnified by existing conflicts in the society or communities hit by a natural disaster. At the same time, the conditions that are at the root of violent conflict often undermine a society's capacity to rebound from a natural disaster, just as they impede efforts at peace building. In addition, in fragile societies or those in transition from war to peace, a natural disaster can often contribute to or exacerbate the underlying causes of violence.

In weak or fragile states, there is often little difference between the consequences—displacement, trauma, etc.—of natural disasters (hurricanes, tsunamis, earthquakes) and those of man-made disasters (war, ethnic cleansing, large-scale rioting). Natural disasters can also contribute to political instability, social (or identity-based) cleavages, economic challenges, food insecurity, and large-scale migration. All of those consequences can, in turn, contribute to greater risk of violence. Economic weakness and a lack of resources reduce a country's ability to meet people's needs. Food insecurity makes it more difficult for a population to remain in a particular locale and contributes to greater health risks, including widespread malnutrition. Large-scale migration often exacerbates weak political conditions, drains economic resources, contributes to cleavages between migrant communities and host communities, and can often spill over into other communities, particularly across borders.

Too often, the consequences and aftermath of a natural disaster negatively reinforce the link between disaster and conflict. A disaster will leave the community poorer, more fragile, and less able to cope with conflict—which, in turn, makes conflict more likely. Natural disasters can combine with other negative changes (poor agriculture harvests, a sudden drop in commodity prices, influxes of refugees, existing demographic pressures, etc.) to put additional strains on already fragile social, economic, and political systems. Additional consequences would include greater unemployment, increased social tension, less access to clean and safe water, and decreased physical security. In countries where poverty, food insecurity, and high levels of unemployment already exist, a natural disaster makes the situation that much worse and more ripe for exploitation by forces involved in conflict.

The Impact of Displacement

One important similarity between wars and natural disasters is that both create significant displacement of populations. Whether displaced by an earthquake or fighting between government forces and paramilitaries, the displaced often lose their livelihoods, possessions, and property; become traumatized; and also lose their family support network. The displaced have similar protection and assistance needs, and often become dependent on governments, aid agencies, charitable groups, or even guerrilla forces. As in wars, the most vulnerable groups are disproportionately affected. For example, globally, for every one adult male who drowns in a flood, there are 3-4 women who die.[7] During wars in the past 20 years, 90% of the victims have been women, children, and the elderly. Sexual abuse and rape of women is often a tool of war, while gender-based violence is unfortunately common among women displaced by both natural disasters and conflict. Displaced children are often more susceptible to recruitment by armed forces. Vulnerable groups also frequently experience discrimination in the provision of

assistance. In many camps where persons displaced by conflict or natural disasters live, food is—at least initially—more likely to go to healthy and strong men than to children or the disabled.[8]

Natural disasters, almost by definition, have environmental effects. But so do conflicts and displacement itself. Refugee camps, for example, can quickly deplete forests in developing countries, which host the majority of the world's refugees. A degraded environment is also more likely to suffer the consequences of natural disasters. For example, Central America's vulnerability to hurricanes and other natural disasters is a product of social, economic, and environmental causes.[9] In addition, the effect of displacement on entire communities is substantial, particularly because shelter, access to food and water, health, and livelihoods are lost. Migration and resulting urbanization put greater strains on the system and make it more difficult to prevent conflict as well as criminality. New immigrants can affect the local economy, land distribution, strains on social services, and the balance of political power and social relations.

One difference between natural disasters and war is that those displaced by natural disasters are, in general, likely to return home more quickly than those displaced by violent conflicts. One of the few studies to systematically compare duration of displacement by its cause found in four South Asian countries that 80% of those displaced by natural disasters had been displaced for one year or less, while 57% of those displaced by armed conflict and 66% of those displaced by development projects had been displaced for more than 5 years.[10] Although systematic data is lacking, people displaced by natural disasters tend to stay within their own country rather than crossing national borders.

The Consequences of Aid and Humanitarian Relief

The role of the military—either national or international forces — in providing assistance to the displaced is more generally accepted in natural disasters than in conflict zones. It is often the case that the military is the national institution most equipped with the logistics, personnel, and supplies to undertake initial rescue and humanitarian response to large disasters. But in conflict-affected countries, the general population often does not trust the military. Ongoing military control of aid and refugee/IDP (internally displaced person) camps can also endanger beneficiaries, because it can heighten the IDPs' vulnerability to sexual exploitation and abuse as well as the military recruitment of children. There is also often suspicion that aid and resources given to disaster victims can be turned over to guerrilla forces and used against the state.

Repressive or weak regimes may interpret spontaneous

Instructional and Classroom Applications

Grade Level: High School

Social Studies Standards
❸ PEOPLE, PLACES, AND ENVIRONMENTS
❾ GLOBAL CONNECTIONS

Scenario

Flooding has caused considerable damage in a remote area of the country. Schools, clinics, and housing have been significantly damaged. Hundreds have died, and many are displaced, adding to the thousands already relocated by ongoing war and poverty. Many residents are angry because authorities have not responded. In the village of Pymara, at least 50 families are displaced, and the school has been completely destroyed. Parents want their children to return to school. The health clinic has suffered considerable damage, and there is fear of flood-related diseases. Local agriculture, a mix of subsistence crops and poppies, has been damaged. Food prices have risen dramatically. Crime has risen.

Two warlords and a national paramilitary group in the area are dedicated to overthrowing the government. The region has periodically been under the control of one or the other in the past three years. Most villagers have little respect for government officials, the military, or police, because most officials are corrupt and treat most in the village as collaborators. There is mounting concern that widespread violence will resume, and many villagers claim that the government is using the flood as an excuse to weaken or eliminate "troublemakers"—those who oppose the authorities. All the while, Pymara has not been able to rebuild the health clinic and school or provide much assistance to the displaced.

Based on the scenario above, divide students into small groups and have them consider the following questions:

▶ What is the nature of the conflict in this region, and how has the flood contributed to the conflict?

▶ What approaches to this natural disaster might help reduce the potential for violent conflict?

▶ What approaches might exacerbate the existing problems, increasing violent conflict?

▶ How important is it to gain the village's support for any plan of action? Why?

disaster relief actions by non-government organizations as threats and respond with repression. At the same time, in the disaster's aftermath, political leaders may try to regain or even enhance their popular legitimacy by exploiting a disaster; they attempt to use disaster relief and recovery to extend their influence over development policies and programs.[11] But that only works if the response is effective. In weak, conflict-ridden societies, that is rarely the case. For internally displaced persons, it is their national governments that are responsible for protecting and assisting them. Governments often do not meet these obligations—whether the precipitating cause of displacement is a hurricane or a civil war.

At the international level, the most common means of response to sudden disasters has often been huge humanitarian relief efforts, but there are consequences to this assistance. The relief efforts do little to help a state improve its own capacity to respond to disaster. If the international relief effort does little to create local capacity, then the populace will continue to place little trust or confidence in the local authorities to handle problems or manage conflicts, thus making conflict more likely. For most of the Cold War, humanitarian relief focused on natural disasters, and where violent conflicts existed, the emphasis was on providing assistance and protection to refugees in neighboring countries. Assistance was provided to all who showed up and were considered as refugees. Neutrality was the watchword; however, in the past decades, it has become clear that the participants of the conflict did not respect declared neutrality and perpetrators began to infiltrate refugee camps, either to recruit combatants, prey on additional victims, or hide from justice under the guise of being a victim.

Humanitarian aid can also create additional problems that contribute to instability and, over the long term, the potential for conflict. With international assistance, recipients may develop a long-term dependence on donors. Development agencies and relief organizations increasingly recognize that it is inadequate and even counterproductive to just deliver things to people. These organizations have moved towards problem solving with countries—otherwise, the countries are simply passive and accepting of aid, while not developing their own institutions and capacity to address local problems. And, even if the aid saves lives and alleviates suffering, it can inadvertently feed into, worsen, and prolong conflict. The most common problem is misappropriation of aid by warring parties. Aid goods are often stolen, taxed at checkpoints, or diverted and manipulated by warring parties for political advantage or profit.

Because of the potential for harm with humanitarian aid, the international community has developed important guidelines and practices. The first document to emerge from the international NGO community in the 1990s was the ten-point Code of Conduct.[12] This was prepared jointly by the International Federation of the Red Cross and Red Crescent Societies and the International Committee of the Red Cross (ICRC), in consultation with the members of the Steering Committee for Humanitarian Response (SCHR).[13] Although the Code of Conduct was envisaged primarily as relating to relief in natural disasters, it has always been seen to apply to NGO humanitarian work in armed conflicts, too. In theory, the Code's articles are now used as key criteria in the planning and evaluation of NGO programming in and around war.

At its core, the guidelines (also referred to as the Sphere Project) promote a humanitarian *imperative*—the right to receive humanitarian assistance. It is a fundamental humanitarian principle that should be enjoyed by all citizens of all countries. Members of the international community recognize an *obligation* to provide humanitarian assistance wherever it is needed. This new emphasis on obligation puts the onus on governments and the donor community not just to provide assistance, but to do so responsibly—in a way that does not fan the flames of conflict. Inherent in this is an understanding that aid can be politicized. Thus, Section 2.4 of the charter notes how the failure of warring parties to respect humanitarian operations and to abuse aid may: "…potentially render civilians more vulnerable to attack, or may on occasion bring unintended advantage to one or more of the warring parties."[14]

What is also significant about the Sphere Project is that there is no distinction between relief for populations displaced by and affected by war or by natural disaster, in large measure because of the recognition that the two are linked. Natural disasters must be viewed within the context of the dynamics of the society that is affected.

Conclusion: Fragile States and Conflict

Natural disasters add to the pressures under which fragile societies live. Poverty, ineffective governance, and social cleavages all undermine the capacity of tenuous societies to respond to a natural disaster. These same factors also contribute to the high risk of violent conflict such a society faces.

For those who study and analyze conflict and peace building, natural disasters are an important subject because they can serve to exacerbate conflict and impede efforts at constructing peace. Without addressing the causes of conflict as well as the aggravating factors that can turn a natural disaster into a trigger for greater

violence, efforts at managing conflict or transforming conflict will be difficult. It is important to understand the causal links and relationships between conflict and humanitarian relief in order to live up to the humanitarian intervention maxim, "Do no harm." It should be noted that victims of natural disasters, even if they are refugees or migrants, are not usually the sources of conflict—they are mostly powerless and marginalized as a result of the disaster. They are usually victims, not threats. But their needs and desperate situations can be exploited by those who are contributing to conflict, and, if the needs and expectations of victims are unmet, they ultimately may take up tools of violence.

If people cannot find clean water for drinking, wood for shelter and fuel, or land for crops, what are the chances that peace will be successful and sustainable? Enhancing the prospects in conflict-affected societies for achieving greater economic development, good governance, rule of law, and enhanced social well-being will lessen, if not eliminate, the prospect of natural disasters exacerbating the potential for violent conflict. 🔊

NOTES
1. Elizabeth Ferris, "Natural Disaster- and Conflict-Induced Displacement: Similarities, Differences and Inter-Connections," speech given at the Brookings Institution, March 27, 2008 (http://www.brookings.edu/speeches/2008/0327).

2. Dawn Brancati, "Political Aftershocks: The Impact of Earthquakes on Intrastate Conflict," *Journal of Conflict Resolution* 51, no.5 (October 2007): 716.

3. Philip Nel and Marjolein Righarts, "Natural Disaster and the Risk of Violent Civil Conflict," *International Studies Quarterly* 52 (2008): 167.

4. Dan Smith and Janani Vivekananda. *A Climate of Conflict: The Links between Climate Change, Peace and War* (London: International Alert, November 2007), p. 12.

5. Travis Nelson, "The Effects of Natural Disaster on Interstate Conflict," paper prepared for the 2008 meeting of the Midwest Political Science Association. www.allacademic.com.

6. Thomas Munita, "A Camp for the Homeless," in *The New York Times* (October 14, 2005): A12.

7. Ferris, *op. cit.*

8. *Ibid.*

9. *Ibid.*

10. *Ibid.*

11. *Ibid.*

12. Sphere Project, *Humanitarian Charter and Minimum Standards in Disaster Response* (Oxford, UK: Oxfam, 2000).

13. Members include Caritas Internationalis, Catholic Relief Services, International Federation of Red Cross and Red Crescent Societies, International Save the Children Alliance, Lutheran World Federation, Oxfam, and the World Council of Churches. The International Committee of the Red Cross has observer status.

14. Sphere Project, *op. cit*, p. 8.

PART 2
CASE STUDIES

OVERLEAF

Aerial View of Flooding South of Dhaka, Bangladesh.

(David Greedy/ Save the Children)

CHAPTER 6

STUDYING THE HAITIAN EARTHQUAKE

WILLIAM R. FERNEKES

THE STUDY OF THE HAITIAN EARTHQUAKE of 2010 and its effects incorporates knowledge from a broad range of disciplines in the social studies. The disaster is, as a result, a very useful topic for issues-based instruction that employs carefully designed lessons, activities, and assessments of student performance. This chapter offers vital information and resources to encourage reflective examination of this event and its consequences for the future of the Haitian people.

Geological, Geographic, and Historical Context

The earthquake that devastated Haiti on January 12, 2010, was the first major earthquake since 1946 to occur in the area of the Caribbean near Puerto Rico, the U. S. Virgin Islands, and Hispaniola (an island shared by Haiti and the Dominican Republic). It registered a magnitude of 7.0. Over the past 500 years, a dozen major earthquakes of this magnitude or higher have struck this area of the Caribbean, a number of which generated destructive tsunamis, such as the one that killed an estimated 1,600 people in 1946.[1]

The U. S. Geological Survey reports that the January 2010 Haiti earthquake resulted from a tectonic plate slip in the boundary region between the Caribbean plate and the North American plate, specifically on what has been termed the Enriquillo-Plantain Garden fault system. This fault system has been associated with four major earthquakes between 1751 and 1860, two of which (1751 and 1770) destroyed the Haitian capitol of Port-au-Prince.[2] Haiti's tropical climate, combined with its relatively rough and mountainous terrain and its legacy of extensive deforestation and soil erosion, make it particularly vulnerable to severe impacts from natural disasters, since the intensity of its rainy season and its susceptibility to violent storms and hurricanes make daily survival difficult when essential services (such as access to potable water) are interrupted or destroyed. The 2010 earthquake registered a magnitude of 7.0, equivalent to approximately 500,000 tons of high explosive. That energy release is comparable to several nuclear bombs.[3] In relative terms, however, this was substantially less than the energy release from the 2004 East Asian earthquake, a magnitude-9.3 event that generated the devastating tsunami that ravaged that region.[4]

Economic, Social, and Political Context

Haiti is the poorest country in the Western Hemisphere, with a population whose life expectancy ranks 181st in the world (59.13 years for males and 62.48 years for females). Eighty percent of the population lives below the poverty threshold, and, while there has been relatively steady economic growth since 2005, Haiti's economy is highly vulnerable to the impact of natural disasters because two-thirds of its labor force works in agriculture, a sector of the economy that suffers disproportionately from severe weather and climatic conditions as well as earthquakes. Widespread deforestation in Haiti has resulted from use of wood for fuel, accelerating the impact of soil erosion and leaving only 28% of the nation's land as arable.[5] Haiti's economy includes a very limited industrial sector (9%) and a gradually expanding service sector (25%), both of which are hampered by the relatively low literacy rate of 52.9% for the country's population.[6]

Since the mid-twentieth century, Haiti's political system has alternated between oppressive dictatorships (such as the rule of the Duvalier family), military rule resulting from coups that removed democratically elected presidents (such as the coups that ousted President Manigat in June 1988, 5 months after his election, and the one that removed President Aristide in 1991), and brief periods of democratic rule, sometimes marked by violence and the assertion of external influence by the United States and international organizations, including the Organization of American States (OAS) and the United Nations (UN), to restore order and sustain democratic rule. With the exception of the period from 2006 to the present (under President Rene Preval), Haiti's population has not experienced a sustained period of political stability rooted in democratic practices, a situation that has hampered efforts to strengthen the nation's infrastructure, improve the quality of life for its citizens, and deepen its commitment to creating a civil society that is less prone to the use of violence and military force as solutions to political conflicts, as well as being less susceptible to external

Electronic Resources for Study of the Haitian Earthquake

Amnesty International, 2010 (January 29). "Haiti's Human Rights Challenge."
www.amnesty.org/en/news-and-updates/haitis-human-rights-challenge-20100129

BBC News—Haiti Devastated by Massive Earthquake.
news.bbc.co.uk/2/hi/8455629.stm

CIA—The World Factbook. "Haiti."
www.cia.gov/library/publications/the-world-factbook/geos/ha.html

Earthquakes—U. S. Geological Survey
earthquake.usgs.gov/earthquakes/

Facts on File News Services. "Country Profile—Haiti."
www.2facts.com

The Guardian (London). "Q & A: Haiti Earthquake." January 14, 2010
www.guardian.co.uk/world/2010/jan/14/haiti-earthquake-questions-and-answers

Haiti Earthquake Clearinghouse
www.eqclearinghouse.org/20100112-haiti/

IRIS—Recent Earthquake Teachable Moments
www.iris.edu/hq/retm

Nature. "Lessons from the Haiti Earthquake."
www.nature.com/nature/journal/v463/n7283/full/463878a.html

PBS Teachers—Resources for the Classroom
www.pbs.org/teachers/connect/resources/7548/preview/

Science Daily. "Major Caribbean Earthquakes and Tsunamis a Real Risk."
www.sciencedaily.com/releases/2005/02/050205102502.htm

Time. "The Haiti Earthquake."
www.time.com/time/specials/packages/0,28757,1953379,00.html

interventions that challenge Haitian sovereignty.

The earthquake of 2010 highlighted the persistent problem of human rights protections in Haiti. Amnesty International identified six persistent human rights concerns.[7] The first issue is child exploitation in situations where children become separated from their parents and other family members. This has led to problems such as illegal adoptions and child trafficking. Second, the issue of lack of security and law enforcement became more intense after the earthquake. Third, millions of people and families were left homeless. As displaced persons, their rights should be protected and they should not be forced to move to areas where they do not want to live. In chapter 11, Walter Kälin (as the Representative of the Secretary General on the Human Rights of Internally Displaced Persons) explains how the human rights of displaced individuals must be considered, since those affected by natural disasters find themselves faced with multiple vulnerabilities. Fourth, violence against women becomes heightened; women and girls may face sexual violence and sex trafficking. Fifth, the increasing number of foreign troops and consultants who arrived in the country must be held accountable to strict rules of engagement. The final issue is the increasing national debt. Though some countries do not expect that Haiti will pay back the funds spent in this disaster, Haiti's long-term debt obligations raise concerns about its future commitment to protecting human rights.

The Haitian Earthquake and its Human Consequences: An Issues-Based Approach

Educators desiring to integrate study of the Haitian earthquake and its consequences within their curricula can profitably apply the ideas offered by Previte in Chapter 15 of this Bulletin. For example, the five types of questions adapted from the Ochoa and Engle framework for issues-based study of natural disasters and human rights can be employed as focus questions for the study of how the Haitian political system, as well as institutions of civil society outside of the formal political system (e. g., nongovernmental organizations), can address challenges to the full range of human rights resulting from the earthquake's impact. Previte notes in Chapter 15 that issues-based approaches can be effective in promoting student reflection about how to prevent and mitigate the impact of future natural disasters, particularly when educators approach these topics as public policy challenges.

Studying the Haitian earthquake appropriately uses a working knowledge of core concepts about natural disasters and how human activity has contributed to their occurrence and to the consequences of the disaster for human societies, other species, and the natural environment. Angus Gunn, in the second chapter of this Bulletin, has provided a detailed explanation of these core concepts, and his discussion of how natural disasters impact urban populations is particularly instructive for Haiti, since the devastation in Port-au-Prince was massive—according to the U.S. Geological Survey on January 12, 2010, the Port-au-Prince area had approximately 222,570 people killed, over 300,000 injured, 1.3 million persons displaced, and close to 100,000 houses destroyed from the earthquake. Gunn's discussion of the scientific and public policy challenges resulting from the impact of natural disasters can help educators make good choices about how to select and organize relevant content, while also suggesting valuable themes for consideration of the long-range implications of natural disasters, such as the development of early warning systems, rapid response networks, and guidelines for urban planning that could lessen the impact of natural disasters on human and animal populations.

A comprehensive set of resources for study of natural disasters and human rights is offered in Chapter 16 of this Bulletin. These can and should be supplemented by ongoing research about the particulars of the Haitian earthquake, its consequences, and connections to human rights protection. The resources cited in this essay can be easily accessed in electronic form, along with the supplementary websites provided in this chapter. More sources are available today than ever before, thanks to widespread Internet accessibility, but it is incumbent upon all social studies educators to carefully critique the sources they choose and evaluate their quality against time-tested, valid criteria. Are the sources based upon sound scholarship? Can the authenticity of the sources be validated and corroborated? Are the sources organized and presented in a coherent, legible, and usable format that makes them accessible to a broad range of students? To what degree do the sources reflect multiple perspectives on the problem or issue under study? These are some of the critical questions that must be answered when making thoughtful choices about content for classroom use, and which are particularly important given access by students to electronic content that is often not effectively critiqued or vetted by authorities prior to its distribution on the Internet.

Lastly, it is essential that educators who use the Haitian earthquake as a case study not engage in what might be termed "comparisons of pain and suffering" between what happened in Haiti and, for example, what resulted from Hurricane Katrina in the United States in 2005. Careful analysis of how different natural disasters occurred and their consequences certainly is warranted, but educators should refrain from engaging students in activities which suggest that populations in one society merit one's compassion or commitment more than another. Strategies that generate hierarchies of pain and suffering have the potential to exclude and marginalize groups who require our utmost attention and concern, and whose human rights are no less important than those with whom we are more familiar, or who are less "foreign" than the students engaged in the unit themselves. The universality of human rights concepts and the likelihood that natural disasters can affect most, if not all, human populations at some time require that study of the Haitian earthquake balance the uniqueness of its geological/geographic and social/economic/political contexts with the universal concepts that serve as the foundation of human rights inquiry in the social studies curriculum. 🔯

NOTES

1. *Science Daily*, February 8, 2005.

2. U. S. Geological Survey: Earthquake Hazards Program. "Magnitude 7.0—Haiti Region 2010 January 12 21:53:10 UTC." earthquake.usgs.gov/earthquakes/eqinthenews/2010/us2010rja6/#summary. Accessed April 11, 2010.

3. *The Guardian* (London), January 14, 2010.

4. *Ibid.*

5. CIA—The World Factbook. "Haiti." www.cia.gov/library/publications/the-world-factbook/geos/ha.html. Accessed 27 April 2010.

6. *Ibid.*

7. Amnesty International, 2010 (January 29). "Haiti's Human Rights Challenge." www.amnesty.org/en/news-and-updates/haitis-human-rights-challenge-20100129. Accessed April 27, 2010.

CHAPTER 7

HURRICANE KATRINA: A TOXIC MIX OF SOCIAL AND GEOGRAPHIC VULNERABILITY

MARGARET SMITH CROCCO AND THOMAS CHANDLER

SEVERAL MONTHS AFTER HURRICANE KATRINA struck in late August 2005, the National Hurricane Center issued this report:

> Katrina was an extraordinarily powerful and deadly hurricane that carved a wide swath of catastrophic damage and inflicted large loss of life. It was the costliest and one of the five deadliest hurricanes to ever strike the United States. Katrina first caused fatalities and damage in southern Florida as a Category 1 hurricane on the Saffir-Simpson Hurricane Scale. After reaching Category 5 intensity over the central coast of Mexico, Katrina weakened to Category 3 before making landfall on the northern Gulf coast. Even so, the damage and loss of life inflicted by this massive hurricane in Louisiana and Mississippi were staggering, with significant effects extending into the Florida panhandle, Georgia, and Alabama. Considering the scope of its impacts, Katrina was one of the most devastating natural disasters in United States history.[1]

The storm drove approximately 1 million people from their homes and caused $100 billion in property damage across an estimated 90,000 square miles in Louisiana, Mississippi, and Alabama.[2] The full extent of the loss of human life may never be known. John Mutter, an international disaster specialist at Columbia University's Earth Institute, notes that getting an accurate count of the dead and missing has been at least as difficult as the challenge of determining the extent of human loss from the Indian Ocean tsunami of 2004 and Pakistani earthquake of 2005. Mutter's most recent estimate places the number of dead or missing from Katrina at over 1,800.[3]

For New Orleans, which sits below sea level, Katrina actually struck twice—first, when the storm made landfall on August 29, 2005; and second, when the levees were breached the next day. Within four and a half hours of Katrina's initial storm surge, the century-old levees system (designed by the Army Corps of

Engineers to protect New Orleans from being engulfed by the surrounding waters of the Mississippi River, Lake Borgne, and Lake Pontchartrain) had been breached in multiple places. By midday on September 1, 2005 (when the waters of Lake Pontchartrain and the city's flooding had reached the same level), 80% of New Orleans lay under water and remained so for weeks.

Hurricane Katrina was both a natural and human-caused disaster. As has been widely noted, its impact on New Orleans depended as much on the failure of engineering, unfulfilled promises of protection, and governmental ineptness as it did on Hurricane Katrina.[4] Indeed, even the White House report on the federal response to Hurricane Katrina, issued in February 2006, acknowledged the government's fault in preventing and addressing the consequences of the storm. Other analysts such as Irwin Redlener, who directs the National Center for Disaster Preparedness, came to the same conclusion, warning Americans of the degree to which the incompetent handling of Hurricane Katrina bodes ill for the country when another "megadisaster" strikes.[5]

To label Katrina a *natural disaster* is misleading since it underplays the longstanding contribution of a set of factors related to politics, policy, and human decision-making to its devastating aftermath. For our purposes, we distinguish natural disasters from human-caused ones since this usage aligns our chapter with so much that has been written about Katrina, even though it differs from the usage in other parts of this Bulletin.

The reasons for the extent of the Katrina catastrophe are multiple. On the one hand, this is a story of geographic vulnerability since so much of New Orleans, especially the newer residential areas outside the French Quarter, lies below sea level. The fragility of these newer residential landscapes has been aggravated by ongoing destruction of the wetlands from exploitation of the region by its petroleum, petrochemical, and shipbuilding industries. Likewise, Louisiana's subsidence at an accelerated pace due to dredging for oil and gas extraction, as well as poorly constructed levees among other factors, contributed significantly to raising the odds of destruction from severe weather events.[6]

On the other hand, this is also a story of social vulnerability, involving race and poverty. The storm preyed upon the old and the poor in its path—most of whom were African American. Race and poverty were key factors in determining who fled New Orleans and who evacuated. Preparedness programs worked reasonably well in some areas (Mississippi and Alabama coasts) but failed miserably in the city of New Orleans. As noted by Cutter and Emrich, "Those with resources left in advance of the approaching hurricane; those without (largely the poor, African Americans, elderly, or residents without private cars) remained, trapped in the rising floodwaters."[7]

Hurricane Katrina provoked unsettling questions among many Americans who witnessed images of their fellow citizens—many of them poor and African American—caught in the flooding, apparently beyond the reach of government help. Worldwide, the media broadcast pictures of individuals seeking rescue from their homes by Coast Guard, private boats, and helicopters. Many Americans and others worldwide asked: How could the most powerful nation in the world seem so ill-equipped to handle a hurricane and its aftermath in a region where violent storms are a predictable seasonal occurrence?

Civic Education: Disasters, Rights, and Hurricane Katrina
Hurricane Katrina and its aftermath can be considered not only a story of geographic and social vulnerability, but also a civic issue to be deliberated by all American citizens. Although it may have been a unique occurrence due to the confluence of climate, geography, politics, and demography, Katrina's implications for the United States demand discussion in classrooms.

The tragedy raises larger questions related to America's identity as a democratic nation, one that not only values personal responsibility but also expects certain things of its government. Analyzing Katrina in this light serves as the basis for a curriculum produced at Teachers College, Columbia University that was built upon Spike Lee's award-winning film, *When the Levees Broke*. The overarching questions posed in the curriculum are: What kind of country are we? What kind of country do we want to be? Thanks to funding by the Rockefeller Foundation, over 30,000 copies of the curriculum have been distributed nationwide to schools, colleges, and community groups.[8] An online copy of the curriculum is available for download at www. teachingthelevees.org.

We encourage educators to use a democratic-dialogue teaching method to explore these issues. Raising questions about controversial issues promotes development of social studies skills such as the critical use of sources, perspective taking, argumentation based on evidence, and reliance on analytical reasoning in support of positions. Each topic introduced here is complex; none affords easy answers. By engaging controversial issues in social studies classrooms, teachers and students bring rational deliberation and civic engagement into citizenship education.[9]

The perspective presented here results from several years investigating these matters in preparing the Teaching *The Levees* curriculum. Teachers engaged in implementing an issues-based social education process may deviate somewhat from the necessarily simplistic sketch presented here. In teaching social issues, teachers or students pose a question, such as those presented here, and then students are guided in seeking evidence, weighing opinions, and considering arguments. Students' answers should be held tentatively and tested against further evidence and competing interpretations. Structuring students' learning experiences in open-ended ways will allow them to reach their own conclusions about these issues, especially the matter of personal and governmental responsibility, more fully explored in the Teaching *The Levees* curriculum.

An Eco-Justice Perspective
An eco-justice framework examines human relations to the earth, taking into consideration issues of equity and fairness in determining who is most vulnerable to environmental catastrophes and why certain groups often experience more harm than others. It also asserts that it is the underserved who tend to experience the most severe long-term consequences from natural disasters, such as those brought on by cataclysmic flooding.[10] Further, Bullard and Wright suggest that the impact of most natural disasters is far from natural, and is rooted in the segregation of impoverished communities from the larger society, both geographically and socially.[11]

Research documents more than 20 years of environmental discrimination in which New Orleans' African American population has been far more negatively affected than other groups. In the early twentieth century, federal policies helped create a racially segregated city. Jim Crow laws, which denied access to education, employment, and public facilities to African Americans, created the first round of trouble; and then, in the second half of the century, the placement of a disproportionate number of polluting industries in African

American communities along Louisiana's portion of the Mississippi River exacerbated the problems based in segregation. Resulting health problems and increased poverty generated what Cutter and Emrich refer to as a set of "social vulnerabilities," or race- and class-based inequalities, which are rarely taken into account during disaster preparedness and response efforts.[12]

In the context of social studies education, a range of curricular subject matter can foster a critical and inclusive understanding of these themes. Comparative studies of poverty and environment may clarify the multiple ways in which different societies prepare for and respond to weather-related risks. For instance, students could consider what other societies have done to address the needs of citizens living in coastal flood-prone urban areas. The Netherlands' experience is particularly noteworthy in this regard, in that much of the nation is below sea level. In February 1953, after a massive storm surge submerged more than 700 square miles of the country, killing 1,835 people, the government vowed that its citizenry would never experience such destruction again. A floodgate made up of two giant arms, each as long as the Eiffel Tower, was then constructed. In the event of a massive storm surge, the barrier automatically closes the waterway, thus shielding Rotterdam, Europe's busiest port, from any damage.[13]

Fast forward to New Orleans in 2010, and the contrast could not be more extreme. It has been five years since Hurricane Katrina devastated the Gulf Coast, and there is still no plan at the federal, state, or local level to consider a new infrastructure project on a par with what has been constructed in the Netherlands.[14] Clearly, students should consider the reasons why this is so, asking, for example: Why isn't the rebuilding of New Orleans deemed a priority in the U.S.? What should be expected of government in protecting its citizenry? Such questions are indispensable in social studies, in that it is the primary area of the curriculum in which the deliberation of contemporary public policy, as well as a commitment to civic engagement, play such a vital role.[15] Unfortunately, for the students involved and for society, resistance exists in many American classrooms to having the kind of meaningful dialogues necessary for addressing these issues. Often when race and class inequalities are central topics, as occurs in much discourse on disasters and human rights, many teachers are reluctant to encourage classroom dialogue. Katrina provides remarkable evidence that race and class remain human and social issues in disasters, a topic worthy of social studies education.

Four issues are among those introduced in the Teaching *The Levees* curriculum:

- ▶ Social vulnerability and Katrina
- ▶ "The Blame Game"
- ▶ Media framing of the tragedy
- ▶ Climate change and New Orleans' future

Consideration of these issues can draw upon the conceptual framework of "eco-justice," the set of ideas that emphasizes our responsibilities as human beings to the rest of the natural world. Each issue is briefly described, then research-based perspectives are offered. Alternative perspectives can and should be developed and examined in classes.

Social Vulnerability and Katrina

What do we know about who died as a result of Katrina? Was any group more vulnerable than another? If so, then why?

Every estimate of the proportion of Katrina's victims in New Orleans who were African American concludes that it was very high. Some estimates put it as high as 91%, and others, at 76%. Of the more than 1,800 dead or missing from Katrina, according to a Katrina List estimate, 914 came from New Orleans. Of the 914 from New Orleans, 830 were African American.[16] The population of New Orleans at the time of Katrina was about two-thirds African American. Some might argue, therefore, that race influenced one's odds of living or dying as a result of the storm.

Even so, flooding affected lower, middle, and upper-middle class neighborhoods. The worst flooded areas included affluent Lakeview, the lower-class but largely home-owning Lower Ninth Ward, and middle-class New Orleans East—all of these were among the 20th century subdivisions made habitable due to the draining of swamps and the building of levees. As historical geographer Richard Campanella commented about Katrina, "The city's ancient geographies of risk, supposedly subjugated by technology a century ago, came rushing back to life."[17]

In addition to the statistical point that a large proportion of dead and missing were African American, more than would be expected based on chance, numerous authors have pointed to poverty's impact, noting, for example, that many poor African Americans did not own cars—about 27% of the adult population, according to Cutter and Emrich.[18] As a result, they were unable to get out of the city on the eve of the storm. Even had they decided to heed the warnings early on (which came from New Orleans' Mayor Ray Nagin too late to be effective, some have argued) and fled on public transportation days before the storm, they lacked credit cards or cash sufficient to secure shelter in suburban hotels. Many poor African Americans were also older, which, in combination with poverty, inhibited their ability to leave. Some older New Orleans citizens also chose to stay because they felt they had successfully weathered previous storms, and so could manage through this one as well.

In the end, 96% of all New Orleans residents evacuated prior to the hurricane, while most of those who stayed lacked the means to leave.[19]

Campanella, who makes a lower estimate than the one cited above of the proportion of Katrina victims who were African Americans, concludes that:

- African Americans made up 67% of New Orleans's population but 76% of its flood victims
- Whites made up 28% of New Orleans's population and 20% of its flood victims
- Hispanics made up 3% of New Orleans's population and 3% of its flood victims
- Asians made up 2% of New Orleans's population and 3% of its flood victims.[20]

He also finds that "African American victims outnumbered white victims by more than double; they comprised 66 percent of the storm deaths in New Orleans and whites made up 31 percent, fairly proportionate to pre-storm relative populations."[21] He goes on to conclude: "There is no question, however, that those who were stranded in the inundated city and suffered excruciatingly long delays in rescue were overwhelmingly African American and poor—in both absolute and relative terms."[22]

A great deal more could be said about the interrelated geographic and social vulnerability of Katrina's victims. Students should surely research these factors along with the city's long history of residential segregation.[23] In the context of Katrina and many other disasters, social vulnerability includes race and class but also may include age, gender, physical ability, and other demographic attributes. All these factors can alter one's risk and raise or lower one's chance of getting assistance after a disaster strikes.[24]

"The Blame Game"

Who was responsible for emergency preparedness in the City of New Orleans? Were preparations sufficient to the task of protecting residents before the storm and rescuing them afterwards? Why or why not?

Given the delayed and widely acknowledged ineffective governmental response to rescue those left behind after Katrina struck, social vulnerability became "social catastrophe":

> The preexisting social vulnerabilities gave rise to the social catastrophe; the moral hazard occurred

with our collective inability to adequately respond. What good is a federal response plan when it clearly does not work and does not alleviate the suffering of the most vulnerable within our society? What does it say about the adequacy of preparedness when we know so little about the most disadvantaged within the communities—those that require additional assistance to get out of harm's way?[25]

Responses to disasters in the United States are supposed to bring intergovernmental cooperation that coordinates the resources of federal, state, and local governments to provide aid.[26] Not only was the federal government's response inadequate but so was that of Mayor Ray Nagin in New Orleans and Governor Kathleen Blanco in Louisiana. Coordinated responses relying on city, state, and national government leave a great deal of room for misunderstanding and misstep, especially when time is of the essence. Even so, some disaster specialists argue that citizens cannot depend for help on the government since it is often unreliable—they must take responsibility for their own preparedness.[27] Once again, we see that tension between personal and governmental responsibility provides an opening for dialogue among students about the "blame game" regarding Katrina.

Many pundits have written that there was plenty of blame to go around. Numerous analyses came to the same conclusion: city and state officials were overwhelmed and at odds, and the federal government's response was delayed, disengaged, and inadequate.[28] But could the damage have been lessened if individuals had taken the warnings more seriously and evacuated as requested? In other words, if 100% of the people evacuated, rather than 96%, would that have made much difference? Is this a reasonable expectation? Can we find evidence from other disasters as a comparison here?

Public and media reactions to the failures of government were sharp and critical. Two out of three Americans believed that President Bush could have done more to speed up relief efforts. In public opinion polls afterwards, the majority of Americans characterized themselves as angry or depressed about the situation. But, once again, race was a factor in shaping opinion—research indicates that African Americans were far more negative about the relief effort than non-African Americans.[29]

One question surfaced repeatedly: If the storm had occurred in an affluent area with a predominantly white population, would the reaction of local, state, and federal governments been different? Such a question, like the one above, could stimulate an interesting comparison of the government's response to other hurricanes in the last 10 years, the forest fires in southern California in 2007, or other similar episodes.

How Did Media Frame the Event?

Did the ways in which American media reported news of Hurricane Katrina and its aftermath bias the story?

Media play a critical role in framing public perception of contemporary events, no less so in the case of Katrina.[30] Prior to Katrina, evidence existed that African Americans have often been presented in a negative light by the news media, as an underclass in American society.[31] The ways in which certain dimensions of a story get emphasized have a profound influence on "what we think about a particular issue."[32] The media's choice, for example, of the word "refugees" to describe individuals displaced by Katrina triggered a fire storm of public reaction. Likewise, rumors circulating about rapes, murders, and general mayhem in the first week after New Orleans flooded, and the use of the term "looting," associated with African Americans, as opposed to "taking," used with Whites, when getting food and other supplies from stores, confirmed for many a belief that the U.S. media was reporting the story of Katrina in a racially biased fashion.[33]

As of September 6, 2005, the Pew Research Center's Project for Excellence in Journalism reported that the topics "Katrina and refugees" could be found in 26,200 articles, "Katrina and looting" in 13,000 articles, and "Katrina and levees" in 13,100. News media around the United States, according to this analysis, doubled their references to both "race" and "African American" over the weekend after Hurricane Katrina struck.

Many scholars who analyzed U.S. coverage found the story of Katrina framed in terms of the poor and African Americans.[34] Differences in media treatment of these issues contributed to shaping views about victimization and Katrina according to one's political worldview.[35] An encouraging development is the adoption by NCSS in 2009 of a position statement about the importance of media literacy.[36] This may lead to greater attention to this important topic in our nation's classrooms.

Climate Change and New Orleans' Future

As noted by climatologist James Hansen, climate change is expected to be one of the most challenging public policy issues of the 21st century.[37] After all, scientific consensus now indicates that the earth's climate is undergoing substantial and, in some cases, alarming changes.[38] Additionally, much of this problem may be irreversible and will only get worse as time goes on.[39]

Without substantial changes in emissions rates, climate change from the buildup of greenhouse gases is likely to lead to extensive transformations of ecosystems and coastlines later this century, thus posing a significant risk to low-lying New Orleans and other coastal areas.[40]

Increased sea-surface temperatures, in return, may be leading to more extreme U.S. weather-related disasters that could destroy flood-prone urban areas that already suffer from significant economic disparities, racism, a lack of health care, and a lack of accessibility to lifelines, such as emergency response personnel, capital, and political representation.[41] Social studies educators' efforts to address these social and geographic vulnerabilities are important since today's learners will be the ones likely to witness and experience climate change's devastating impact on the U.S. Within a social studies context, discussion of climate change—in terms of both mitigation and adaptation—becomes one of citizenship, in which learners are faced with hard questions, such as: Am I a part of the problem, or part of the solution? Why are some of my elected officials still denying that there is even a problem, when the scientific consensus suggests that doing nothing will result in catastrophe? How is media framing these issues in their reporting?"

As shown by Hurricane Katrina, several coastal urban areas of American cities possess significant geographic and social vulnerabilities, the latter often due to inequalities involving race and class. Within such locations, thousands of citizens live in flood-prone areas without any means to evacuate from major storms and no disaster plan to guide them when a megadisaster occurs.[42] Rozario asserts that catastrophic floods, and our discourses about them, have played a long and influential role in the construction of American identities, power relations, economic systems, and environmental practices.[43] What if increased sea-surface temperatures lead, as predicted, to rising tides and more extreme weather-related disasters in low-lying areas? Who is responsible for ensuring that such events will have a limited impact on American society's most vulnerable?[44] Are there aspects of our historical and cultural worldview about the earth and its relation to human life that are inhibiting our ability to deal with these problems effectively?

U.S. politicians are beginning to take note of climate change and its implications for public policy, albeit rather slowly. For instance, while speaking at the National Press Club in Washington, DC, on July 29th, 2008, House Majority Whip James Clyburn, D-S.C., noted:

It is critical [that] our community be an integral and active part of the debate because African-Americans are disproportionately impacted by the effects of climate change economically, socially, and through our health and wellbeing.[45]

Rep. Clyburn further commented that the U.S. African American population is more vulnerable to higher energy bills, unemployment, and recessions caused by global energy price shocks than other groups. He sees Hurricane Katrina's impact on New Orleans as a preview of coming problems for such communities. Such comments remind us that "natural disasters" have less to do with nature than with equity and fairness. Their inclusion in social studies education needs to be a primary aim. Social studies scholars and teacher educators have begun to call—once again—for more attention to these issues in citizenship education.[46] Such calls echo earlier efforts at "greening America" through the social studies.[47]

Conclusion

Geographic and social vulnerability converged in various ways during Hurricane Katrina and its aftermath, producing an American disaster. The issues briefly explored here include the ways in which environmental degradation, government failure in protecting its citizens, and the role of media in shaping public opinion all interacted with those vulnerabilities to produce a toxic mix. Drawing upon an eco-justice framework, teachers can pose critical questions and encourage democratic dialogue about these issues in ways that enhance students' social studies knowledge and skills.

Katrina was a major tragedy in American history. Recent reports about the civic outlook of the Millennial Generation (the large and rising group of young people born between 1978 and 2000) give us optimism that the issues around Katrina will be acknowledged and debated.[48] We call upon social studies educators to provide space for young people to consider what's at stake in our collective futures from the threats of such disasters and what we can do as individuals and as a nation to better address these risks. 🖎

NOTES
1. Richard Knabb, Jamie Rhome, and Daniel Brown, "Tropical Cyclone Report: Hurricane Katrina, National Hurricane Center," *Fire Engineering* 105, no. 5 (2006): 32.

2. James R. Elliot and Jeremy Pais, "Race, Class, and Hurricane Katrina: Social Differences in Human Responses to Disaster," *Social Science Research* 35: 295-321; Sean O'Keefe, "Looking Back, Moving Forward," *Public Administration Review 6 (2006):* 5-21.

3. "The Katrina List," www.katrinalist.columbia.edu.

4. *Levees.org*, an organization dedicated to holding the Army Corps of Engineers responsible for the failure of the levees in Hurricane Katrina, called this engineering failure second only to the failure of the nuclear power plant at Chernobyl in the Ukraine (then part of the Soviet Union) in 1986. See levees.org.

5. Irwin Redlener, *Americans at Risk* (New York: Knopf, 2006).

6. Ivor van Heerden and M. Bryan, *The Storm* (New York: Penguin, 2006).

7. Susan L. Cutter and Christopher Emrich, "Moral Hazard, Social Catastrophe: The Changing Face of Vulnerability Along the Hurricane Coasts," *The Annals of the American Academy of Political and Social Science 604,* no. 1 (2006): 105.

8. Margaret S. Crocco, *Teaching* The Levees*: A Curriculum for Democratic Dialogue and Civic Engagement* (New York: Teachers College Press, 2007).

9. Joseph Kahne and Joel Westheimer, "The Limits of Political Efficacy: Educating Citizens for a Democratic Society," *PS: Political Science and Politics 39,* no.2: 289-96; Diana Hess, *Controversial Issues in Classrooms* (New York: Routledge, 2009).

10. Chet Bowers, "Towards an Eco-justice Pedagogy," *Educational Studies 32,* no. 4: 401-16; Rebecca Martusewicz, *Seeking Passage: Post-structuralism, Pedagogy, Ethics* (New York: Teachers College Press, 2001).

11. Robert Bullard and Beverly Wright, *Race, Place, and Environmental Justice after Hurricane Katrina: Struggles to Reclaim, Rebuild, and Revitalize New Orleans and the Gulf Coast* (Boulder, CO: Westview Press, 2009).

12. Cutter and Emrich, "Moral Hazard, Social Catastrophe: The Changing Face of Vulnerability Along the Hurricane Coasts," 106.

13. David Wolman, "Before the Levees Break: A Plan to Save the Netherlands," *Wired Magazine,* no. 17.01 December, 2008. Accessed at www.wired.com/science/planetearth/magazine/17-01/ff_dutch_delta.

14. Thomas Chandler, *Civic Engagement About Climate Change: A Case Study of Three Educators and Their Practice.* Ph.D. dissertation. Teachers College, Columbia University, 2009.

15. Crocco, *Teaching* The Levees.

16. The Katrina List, www.katrinalist.columbia.edu.

17. Richard Campanella, "An Ethnic Geography of New Orleans," *Journal of American History 94,* no. 3 (2007): 704-715.

18. Cutter and Emrich, "Moral Hazard, Social Catastrophe: The Changing Face of Vulnerability Along the Hurricane Coasts."

19. *Ibid.*

20. Campanella, 712.

21. *Ibid.,* 714

22. *Ibid.,* 715

23. See, for example, John R. Logan, *The Impact of Katrina: Race and Class in Storm-damaged Neighborhoods.* Unpublished manuscript. Spatial Structures in the Social Sciences Initiative, Brown University, 2006. Accessed on June 8, 2009, at www.s4.brown.edu/katrina/report.pdf.

24. Bullard and Wright, *Race, Place, and Environmental Justice after Hurricane Katrina: Struggles to Reclaim, Rebuild, and Revitalize New Orleans and the Gulf Coast.*

25. Cutter and Emrich, 105.

26. Saundra Schneider, "Who's to Blame? (Mis)perceptions of the Intergovernmental Response to Disasters," *Publius: The Journal of Federalism 38,* no. 4 (2008): 615-738.

27. Gregory Thomas, *Freedom from Fear (*New York: Random House, 2005).

28. See, for example, Douglas Brinkley, *The Great Deluge: Hurricane Katrina, New Orleans, and the Mississippi Gulf Coast* (New York: HarperCollins, 2006); Jed Horne, *Breach of Faith: Hurricane Katrina and the Near Death of a Great American City* (New York: Random House, 2006); and Schneider, "Who's to Blame? (Mis)perceptions of the Intergovernmental Response to Disasters."

29. Donald P. Haider-Markel, William Delehanty, and Matthew Beverlin, "Media Framing and Racial Attitudes in the Aftermath of Katrina." *The Policy Studies Journal 35*, no. 4 (2007): 587-605.

30. *Ibid.*

31. See, for example, Martin Gilens, "Race and Poverty in America: Public Misperceptions and the American News Media," *Public Opinion Quarterly 60* (1996), no. 4: 515-41; T.A. Satterfield, C. K. Mertz and P. Slovic, "Discrimination, Vulnerability, and Justice in the Face of Risk," *Risk Analysis 24*, no.1 (2004): 115.

32. Gilens, 293.

33. Aaron Kinney, "Looting" or "finding." Salon.com (September 1, 2005).

34. Leonie Huddy and Stanley Feldman, "Worlds Apart: Blacks and whites React to Hurricane Katrina," *Du Bois Review 3*, no. 1: 97-113.

35. Kathryn A. Sweeney, "The Blame Game: Racialized Responses to Hurricane Katrina," *Du Bois Review 3*, no. 1 (2006): 161-174.

36. See the NCSS Position Paper on Media Literacy at www.socialstudies.org/positions/medialiteracy.

37. James E. Hansen, "Global Warming Twenty Years Later: Tipping Points Briefing Before the Select Committee on Energy Independence and Global Warming, U.S. House of Representatives." 2008. Retrieved October 8, 2008, from www.columbia.edu/~jeh1.

38. Intergovernmental Panel on Climate Change, "The Physical Science Basis Contribution of Working Group I to the Fourth Assessment Report of the Intergovernmental Panel on Climate Change." Retrieved April 10, 2008, from ipcc-wg1.ucar.edu/wg1/docs/WG1AR4_SPM_Approved_05Feb.pdf.

39. Bill McKibben, *The Bill McKibben Reader* (New York: Henry Holt and Company, 2008).

40. Hansen, "Global Warming Twenty Years Later: Tipping Points Briefing Before the Select Committee on Energy Independence and Global Warming, U.S. House of Representatives."

41. Susan L. Cutter, Bryan J. Boruff, and W. Lynn Shirley, "Social Vulnerability to Environmental Hazards," *Social Science Quarterly 84*, no. 1 (2003): 242-261.

42. Donald Brown, *White Paper on the Ethical Dimensions of Climate Change* (EDCC, Rock Ethics Institute, Pennsylvania State University, University Park, PA, 2006).

43. Kevin Rozario, *The Culture of Calamity: Disaster and the Making of Modern America* (Chicago: University of Chicago Press, 2007).

44. Brown, *White Paper on the Ethical Dimensions of Climate Change, 2008.*

45. Jeff Poor, House Majority Whip, "Climate Change Hurts Blacks More." *Business & Media Institute,* July 29, 2008.

46. Neil Houser, "Ecological Democracy: An Environmental Approach to Citizenship Education," *Theory and Research in Social Education 37*, no. 2 (2009): 192-215.

47. See, for example, the chapter by Stephen Fleury and Adam Sheldon, "Environmentalism and Environmental Issues," in Ronald W. Evans and David Warren Saxe, Eds., *Handbook on Teaching Social Issues* (Washington, DC: National Council for the Social Studies, 1996): 188-196.

48. Data on the political ideology of contemporary American youth can be found at www.americanprogress.org/issues/2009/05/political_ideology_youth.html. For more on the importance of such attitudes, see Peter Levine, *The Future of Democracy: Developing the Next Generation of American Citizens* (Lebanon, NH: Tufts University Press, 2007).

CHAPTER 8

POVERTY AND NATURAL DISASTERS IN NEPAL

BINAYA SUBEDI

WHAT IMAGES ARE MOST LIKELY COME TO YOUR MIND if you are asked to imagine the country of Nepal? It is likely that you will imagine Mt. Everest. Or you may even talk about how cows are considered sacred in the country. You may talk about a visual you may have seen of crowded streets of a city that looked like a "different" or an archaic setting. Or you may talk about the natural beauty of the country and how you may have thought about traveling there. You may not be familiar with the society, but such images will have shaped your prior knowledge about Nepal.

Much of the information that we receive about Nepal in the mainstream media, including what is written in textbooks, comes through mainstream sources. Clearly, mainstream knowledge does not provide complex perspectives on a given issue on culture and history. Various scholars have pointed out how the media, along with the formal school curriculum, shape students' perceptions about global societies.[1]

Considering that non-western countries are often viewed in stereotypical terms,[2] there are pedagogical complexities associated with discussing natural disasters in social studies classrooms. One may ask: What if the very discussion about natural disasters reinforces stereotypes about marginalized societies within the framework of problem stories? Readers may further interpret how societies such as Nepal are incapable or irresponsive to natural disasters. Or worst, readers may be led to believe that a society's incapability has to do with its "way of life" or cultural practices. Considering the difficulties of translating such topics across cultures, this chapter proposes the need to learn critically about global poverty so that educators can better understand how economically underprivileged people face or cope with natural disasters. Questions on international dimensions of poverty are often marginalized when conceptualizing the notion of global citizenship. Considering that it is through sheer luck that we are born in a particular geography or socio-economic status, we need to consider our global responsibilities in a more critical way.[3] Currently, millions of children around

the world are living in chronic poverty and find it difficult to make a living.[4] When we learn to value learning about chronic poverty, we can better understand the context in which people encounter natural disasters. First, the examination of global poverty helps us recognize the context in which people live and face difficult circumstances. Secondly, the examination of global poverty helps us recognize how broader socio-political issues are connected to how or why people encounter natural disasters.

Stories of Nepal

Two stories that are often written about Nepal are about landslides (or mud slides) and famine. Clearly, there are multiple topics that we can analyze to look at socio-economic issues in Nepal. Research indicates that whenever stories on global poverty and complex cultural issues are talked about in classrooms, they are often met with humor or stereotypes.[5] Social studies curricula are often silent on addressing critical topics such as natural disasters and the complex ways such events impact people. Newspapers in the United States generally do not cover Nepal on a consistent basis, with the exception of stories on the devastating impact of landslides or food shortages. The descriptions of these disasters are tragic (i.e., family possessions being washed away) and often difficult to read—people being buried alive, children being unaccounted for, and, in many cases, parents or grand-parents out-living their children or grand children. These accounts are highly visible since they are published in various newspapers.[6] Yet, they are also invisible since they are addressed in a marginal way and often function to reveal the "problems" in Third World societies.

Poverty and Natural Disasters

Nepal is an economically underprivileged nation-state and is often placed within the category of LDC (Least Developed Countries). According to the United Nations, it ranks as one of the poorest countries in the world.[7] There is a small middle class. It is estimated that one third of the population lives in deep, chronic poverty and struggles to meet everyday needs. Poverty operates in both individual/family and structural contexts, and impacts people or communities in everyday contexts. For instance, families who live in chronic poverty have to find food or shelter or may need financial resources to travel for medical care. Poverty is structural in the sense that LDCs face enormous odds in eliminating poverty due to the lack of resources, industrial capabilities, and technological knowledge that people possess. Countries like Nepal often face the pressure to economically modernize and be part of the world economic system, yet the rules of the world economic system do not favor LDCs. For instance, even when loans might be offered from the International Monetary Fund or the World Bank to fight poverty, LDCs struggle to even pay interest on such loans, and this plunges such countries into an unending debt cycle.[8] The reality of poverty makes the path to economic prosperity incredibly difficult. The sheer fact that 50% of Nepali people (most of whom reside in rural areas) are unable to read or write makes poverty a difficult reality to combat.[9]

In virtually all countries, economic poverty is prevalent in urban areas as well as rural areas. In the Nepali context, rural poverty has been historically marginalized. When cities modernized over the last thirty years, people in rural areas often did not have access to equal opportunities in areas such as education, transportation, health care, etc. There are a number of reasons for the rural neglect. First, people in larger cities have historically welded power and resources to rule the country. Their interest, too often, was maintaining power by managing larger populated areas. Although there is poverty in larger cities, the poverty in rural areas is spread across a larger geographical area since a majority of the population lives in rural areas and relies on agriculture as a way of making a living.[10] Second, the lack of roads and bridges in rural areas has played a major role in maintaining the cycle of poverty. The physical landscape (particularly in the northern part of the country) is rugged and mountainous, and building roads and bridges has always been difficult, costly, and (sadly) marginalized. Because of the geographical difficulties, people in rural areas have historically been isolated, and the government has had difficulties in providing essential services such as hospitals, schools, roads, etc., to people in rural areas. Nepal has not had the economic means to build roads, hospitals, schools, and bridges across the country. And whenever it has had resources to invest in specific geographical areas, too often rural areas have not been a priority.[11]

The Impact of Landslides

It has been reported that more than 1,000 people die each year in Nepal because of natural disasters, and flooding and landslides are the leading causes of human death.[12] A story published in a Nepali newspaper with the headline "Landslides Claim Six Lives in Kaski and Mugu" wrote:

> At least six people have died and two more have gone missing in separate landslide-related incidents in various parts of the country caused by incessant rainfall from the past few days. Three members of a family died when a house was swept away by a mudslide at Deurali VDC-8, Kaski district. The deceased have been identified as Mangali Gurung, 80, Soni Gurung, 25, and one and a-half-year old Purnima Gurung, according to Kaski district police. Rekha Gurung, 11, who was swept away along with the house, was rescued from the banks of a nearby river. Another two members of the house, Sim Bahadur Gurung and his wife, were not in the house when the tragedy struck and are reported to be safe.[13]

An examination of local papers in Nepal reveals that landslides (with accompanying tragedies) are common in rural areas during the monsoon season. These stories help us understand a number of issues. First, landslides or mudslides are both natural and unnatural disasters. They are *natural* in the sense that they are unpredictable and often triggered by incessant rain. This is particularly true in monsoon seasons when there is heavy rainfall, often for days. For people in rural areas, who rely on rain for agriculture, heavy rain can be catastrophic. For homes that do not have solid foundations, heavy rain can mean the loss of a living space and, sadly, the loss of lives, taking a heavy toll on the people who are the most vulnerable and economically underprivileged in a society.

In many cases, landslides take place because of the loss of trees in a region, since trees are known to hold soil and prevent mudslides. When families cut trees and collect wood for the purpose of cooking, such a practice doesn't necessarily impact the shifting of soil. However, when national and transnational business entities systematically eliminate forests, it does have a devastating impact on the nature of the landslide that may take place. Too often, business entities have been complicit in the deforestation of vast regions of Nepal, and the wood has been sold in the international markets.[14] This is not simply an issue about trees; the habitats for endangered species and plants that have medicinal potential have also been destroyed.

A related topic concerns the categories of gender and childhood. In rural areas in Nepal, natural disasters impact women and children in profound ways. Because of economic poverty, men from rural areas often move to cities to look for employment. The practice of having family members working in the city and sending money home is very common in Nepal. In rural areas of western Nepal, it is not uncommon to hear stories of how young men and women have moved to cities in India and Nepal. In recent years, thousands of Nepali people have sought work as manual laborers in East Asia or the Middle East.[15] Although men are migrating because of poverty, women continue to live in rural areas to take care of homes, families, and farms. Sadly, women often face a disproportionate burden of dealing with tragic events such as landslides and food shortages. Children often become victims of disasters, and the premature death of children in rural areas raises questions about the extent to which the government has been effective in preventing or mitigating natural disasters.

Many accounts of landslides and food shortages in Nepal speak of how rescue workers or medical personnel have had difficulty reaching rural locations. In many cases, there may not be paved or dirt roads on which to travel, or some areas may only be accessible by small planes (following which, there is a need to walk to the location, often for days). This issue of access speaks of how necessary infrastructure (such as roads, bridges, etc.) is often lacking in rural areas. Most Nepali villages and towns are not accessible by motor vehicles. To reach paved roads in Nepal, it's estimated that 37% of households have to walk 30 minutes and 27% of the population has to walk three hours.[16]

Roads are rare in mountainous areas, and people often use small bridges (for human travel only) to cross ravines and rivers. Yet, when a bridge is destroyed by a landslide, the relief effort becomes even more difficult. The construction of narrow bridges (known as trail bridges) has helped relief efforts and made mobility easier and safer across hills or ravines. The lack of a bridge may have meant climbing difficult terrains or crossing dangerous rivers. Although cars can't travel on bridges in mountainous areas, they serve an important function in the everyday travel of people to markets, to obtain water, or to travel to nearby towns. These failures of governmental policies demonstrate how disasters continue to impact the rural poor disproportionately.

Infrastructure and Safety Net

The lack of bridges (for vehicles) and roads means that the quick movement of people and goods is severely restricted, particularly during a time of disaster. Without infrastructure, it becomes difficult for communities to trade goods from rural areas to cities in a systematic way. Historically, rural communities have created markets in various regions to buy and sell products. But during times of crisis and whenever there is an immediate need, without roads or bridges, quick access to a community becomes difficult. Historically, most rural communities have remained economically self-sufficient, but during times of severe crisis they are in need of assistance. The lack of infrastructure further isolates communities during times of crisis, thus perpetuating an impediment to responding to various forms of national tragedies.

Famine is particularly acute in the western part of Nepal where there is extreme poverty. On a yearly basis, stories of systematic famine are widely circulated in the media. Since a majority of the population relies on farming as a way of making a living, natural disasters such as droughts and flooding severely impact people's ability to make a living. Once again, the lack of roads and bridges in rural areas hampers efforts to distribute food and medical supplies in a timely manner.

Whenever there is a food shortage, it clearly impacts mothers and children, particularly a newborn who may not have access to proper nutrients. Even during times when there are no recorded natural disasters, the infant mortality rate has remained high in Nepal. In 2009, the World Health Organization estimated that there were 61 deaths for every 1,000 live births in Nepal.[17] Furthermore, of the estimated 50,000 children who die in Nepal annually, 60% of that total is attributed to malnutrition. Such a high rate of infant death is directly connected to rural poverty, particularly the lack of hospitals, nurses, or medical professionals in rural areas. Clearly, when natural disasters strike in economically underprivileged areas, they make conditions even more difficult for people.

Unlike many industrialized nation-states, Nepal does not have a "safety net" in place that allows flood victims or people who have been affected by food shortages to seek compensation from the government. In industrialized countries, people may be able to seek grants from the government to rebuild homes and farms after a particular disaster. Alternatively, they might be able to file for unemployment compensation. The Nepali government has historically not been able to provide such forms of assistance due to the fact that the government has had neither the monetary ability nor a system in place to assist victims of such disasters. Economically underprivileged people have neither the access

Instructional and Classroom Applications

There are several ways students in middle or high school can examine the relationship between poverty and natural disasters. Students can examine topics in areas of economics (**⑦ PRODUCTION, DISTRIBUTION, AND CONSUMPTION**) or in relation to geography (**❸ PEOPLE, PLACES, AND ENVIRONMENTS**). For instance, both areas can be integrated in studying the United Nations Millennium Goals to eradicate poverty by 2015 and the kinds of issues they outline as being important to reduce global poverty. Students can examine how the goals are being met and what local communities are doing to work against land erosion or food shortages. Or, for instance, students can examine how the construction of trail bridges has helped people's ability to move across mountainous terrains.

To extend the lesson on economics, students can examine to what extent industrialized nation-states are assisting countries such as Nepal. For instance, students can examine to what extent the United States allocates funds for the prevention of natural disasters or the building of infrastructure that would alleviate poverty. Another way of extending the study is by examining newspaper accounts of natural disasters and monitoring what areas are being impacted. In particular, students can examine the impact of a particular disaster on women, children, and marginalized groups. Students ought to send their reports to national and international leaders and advocate that the industrialized nations assist in providing financial and technical support in the building of infrastructures in various parts of the world. Students' reports should demonstrate critical thinking abilities and include evaluations of particular events, current policies, and policy recommendations.

nor ability to purchase insurance that would allow people to seek compensation. Privileged people who live in larger cities may be able to afford insurance, but this is simply beyond the reach of most Nepali people.

Human Rights: Economics, Ethnicity, and Gender

In the United States, studies indicate that 10% of the population owns 90% of the resources.[18] This uneven allocation of wealth is a global phenomenon. In Nepal, much of the land is controlled by wealthy people, most of who live in cities and rent land to farmers. In most cases, farmers live on the farm, and farmers who work the land get limited compensation from the owners based on what's being produced on the land. When natural disasters take place, the burden of the loss of crops is often placed on the farmers, and too often this further increases the amount of money that they would owe to landowners.[19]

When events such as flooding, droughts, or landslides occur, this places incredible burdens on farmers who have to rework the land. This is particularly true of rugged terrains where farming is difficult to begin with. In Nepal, virtually all forms of farming are conducted with traditional methods relying primarily on manual labor. Once again, technological equipment or tractors are simply beyond the financial reach of farmers. In rural areas, productive seeds and fertilizers are also difficult to obtain because farmers simply do not have the means to buy them.

Because of the lack of resources, the planting and harvesting of crops is labor intensive. Families often have to make a hard decision to either send their children to school or have them work in the fields. In Nepal, poverty is high in areas where there are no or limited schooling options. Education becomes a vehicle that can give marginalized people access to jobs and also provides a means to question societal practices.

The predicament faced by farmers is directly connected to broader issues of land rights in Nepal. Historically, ownership of land has been a contested issue since women, people of marginalized ethnicities, and indigenous people have been denied access to the ownership of land. Also, marginalized communities have had limited access to arable land in the country. In many cases, people in power (men of privileged ethnic backgrounds) usurped land that had historically belonged to indigenous groups, and land was often divided among privileged communities. The call for a more equitable (re)allocation of land is not simply a political issue but is connected to the difficult economic conditions faced by people.[20]

In patriarchal societies, land and properties have often been inherited by or sold to a male person. Historically, in Nepal, only men could be legal landowners or home owners. Subsequently, laws gave men more power over socio-economic domains, and women were not able to have equal access to education or health care.

Disasters place particular demands on women, who often find themselves working at home and in the fields. Outside the cities, it is fairly common to see women working in the fields, often in knee-deep water planting rice or corn, with children strapped on their backs. The necessity to work often compromises schooling options for women, who find it difficult to balance home/field obligations and attending school. Such conditions have further reinforced gender inequities in Nepal.[21]

Gender plays a critical role in examining land issues and natural disasters. When women become more formally educated in rural areas, they are more likely to seek options to make their (and their family's) lives better. Yet, family obligations or safety concerns often hinder women's desires to move to regions that are less prone to natural disasters. Poverty is one of the main reasons that forces women to migrate to cities.

In the last two decades, women have sought more political and economic rights through participation in various social groups and political processes.[22] By participating in various non-governmental organizations, women have advocated more control over how policies and laws are being developed that would meet the needs of women, particularly for women who are economically underprivileged and not formally educated.

The political mobilizations of women and people of marginalized ethnicities have made questions of human rights more visible in Nepali politics in recent years. The emphasis on human rights has highlighted the marginalized conditions of underprivileged women and the policies and laws necessary to bring about social change. These are an important part of the social, political and economic context in which people in Nepal have responded to natural disasters. 🐾

NOTES

1. Michael Apple, *Cultural Politics and Education* (New York: Teachers College Press, 1996); Richard Dyer, *The Matter of Images: Essays on Representations* (New York: Routledge, 2002).

2. Edward Said, *Covering Islam* (New York: Vintage Books, 1997).

3. Martha Nussbaum, *Cultivating Humanity* (Cambridge, MA: Harvard University Press, 1997).

4. UNICEF, *Annual Report* (New York: United Nations Publications, 2008), 5-17.

5. Binaya Subedi, "Fostering Critical Dialogue across Cultural Differences: A Study of Immigrant Teachers' Interventions in Diverse Classrooms," *Theory and Research in Social Education* 36, no. 4 (2008): 413-40.

6. United Nations Country Team, *Annual Report: United Nations Development Assistance Framework for Nepal* (Kathmandu, Nepal: United Nations Office, 2008).

7. United Nations Development Programme (UNDP), Nepal Human Development Report, 2007/08. Accessed on August 1, 2009, from hdrstats.undp.org/countries/country_fact_sheets/cty_fs_NPL.html.

8. Jeffrey Sachs, *Common Wealth: Economics for a Crowded Planet* (New York: Penguin, 2008).

9. UNICEF, Nepal Report (2009). Accessed on July 15, 2009, from www.unicef.org/infobycountry/nepal_nepal_background.html.

10. Kamal Rak Dhugel, *Readings in Nepalese Economy* (Vedams: New Delhi, 2004).

11. Nanda R. Shrestha, *In the Name of Development: A Reflection on Nepal* (University Press of America: Lanham, Maryland, 1997).

12. "NEPAL: Huge Challenges in Preparing for Natural Disasters," IRIN News (October 8, 2008). Retrieved on August 1, 2009, from www.alertnet.org/thenews/newsdesk/IRIN/261e7d08284657cf03b0fd6bb28518dd.htm.

13. "Landslides Claim Six Lives in Kaski and Mugu," Nepalnews.com (July 2, 2009). Accessed on July 19, 2009, from www.nepalnews.com/main/index.php/news-archive/19-general/266-landslides-claim-six-lives-in-kaski-and-mugu.html.

14. Shrestha, 1997.

15. D. Seddon, J. Adhikari, and G. Gurung, "Foreign Labor Migration and the Remittance Economy of Nepal," *Critical Asian Studies* 34, no. 1 (March 2002): 19-40.

16. Central Bureau of Statistics, *Nepal Living Standards Survey: Statistical Report* (Kathmandu: Nepal, 2003/2004).

17. World Health Organization. *World Health Statistics.* (Geneva, Switzerland: World Health Organization, 2009), 14.

18. Allan G. Johnson, *Privilege, Power and Difference* (New York: McGraw-Hill, 2001).

19. Nanda R. Shrestha, *The Political Economy of Land, Landlessness, and Migration in Nepal* (Kathmandu, Nepal: Nirala Press, 2001).

20. Devi Prasad Kandel, *Property Rights of Women in Nepal* (Kathmandu: Ratna Pustak, 2005).

21. Samira Luitel, *Women in Development* (Nayabazar: Karnali Offset Printing, 1992).

22. Sheila Rowbotham and Stephanie Linkogle, ed., *Women Resist Globalization: Mobilizing for Livelihood and Rights* (London & New York: Zed Books, 2001).

CHAPTER 9

NATURAL DISASTERS IN THE LIVES OF WOMEN LIVING IN POVERTY IN SOUTHERN AFRICA

MAVIS B. MHLAULI, BETHANY VOSBURG-BLUEM, AND MERRY M. MERRYFIELD

AUTHORS' NOTE: *The African Union is an organization of 53 nation-states in Africa with the goals of protection of human rights, advancement of democracy, and supporting economic development. The organization bears witness to the African Charter on Human Rights and Peoples' Rights. These rights include the right of equal protection under the law, the right to work, and the right to an education. The Rights of Women in Africa, another important document, was ratified and/or signed by nations in southern Africa, such as Lesotho, Mozambique, Namibia, South Africa, Swaziland, Zimbabwe, and Zambia. The women described in this piece are strong, hard-working primary caregivers who live in poverty. We believe that students in the United States need to learn about their lives, appreciate their strength and determination, and reflect on the contextual factors that influence their decisions. Materials in this piece can be used to develop open-mindedness, perspective consciousness (putting oneself into the perspectives, knowledge, and experiences of others), and an analysis of culture and experiences as they impact people's decisions and world views. Ideas presented here can also be used to counter the negative and stereotypical media images of women in Africa as helpless, pitiful, or impotent. Although these women face severe economic challenges, they have agency, knowledge, and skills that merit study and respect.*[1]

WHEN NATURAL DISASTERS STRIKE, people are not equally vulnerable. Researchers have found that across the planet, women living in poverty, especially those who are heads of their households, are especially at risk. Worldwide, women make up 70% of the people living in absolute poverty. Although women contribute 66% of the world's work hours and produce 50% of the world's food, they earn only 10% of the world's income and own less than 1% of the world's property.[2] Poverty has considerable impact on survival after a natural disaster, as women who are pregnant or lactating, chronically undernourished, illiterate, residing in substandard housing, or living hand to mouth have few options when natural disasters happen.

Women have higher mortality rates than men during disasters because of the intersections of society's norms and economic realities. When faced with a drought or earthquake, women continue their roles as primary caregivers to the young and the very old. It is often a woman who stays behind to protect fragile elders or try to save the few resources that are her sole means of support—a grainery, farm animals, a structure, or goods. These actions make sense, given women's work. The global economic reality is that 70% of the world's women hold jobs in the informal economy, so their income depends on selling produce or prepared food or other products on the street or in small markets, or providing services to others such as cleaning or farming. Natural disasters put them at high risk of losing both their family's shelter and their means of making a living.

Social, religious, or political norms often place restrictions on where women can go, what they must wear in public, and with whom they can interact, so that during a disaster, women are unprepared to seek out help or unsure of how to deal with government officials or aid workers. Being female brings personal vulnerability as rape and violence escalate during crises. Women who leave their homes and are perceived by others to be entering "men's" places (a garage, a coffee house, a beer hall, a construction site) may find themselves at risk.

Women's vulnerability does not end when the natural disaster is over. Intersections of gender, culture, politics, and poverty are powerful factors in how disasters affect a community and who manages to get help. Because families headed by women are often economically, culturally, and politically disadvantaged, they may be overlooked in disaster relief as it is usually headed up by men and privileged male heads of households.[3]

This chapter is a starting point for the study of women and natural disasters, with a focus on Southern Africa. The first section identifies ways in which natural disasters affect women's lives and illustrates some of the major issues and problems. The second section examines how women work to overcome the effects of disasters and improve their lives. The chapter concludes with lesson ideas for teaching about natural disasters in the context of women's lives in Southern Africa.

How Are Women Affected by Natural Disasters?

At the core of women's lives in Southern Africa is the responsibility of feeding and caring for their families. As seen in Table 1, the most common natural disasters in southern Africa are floods, epidemics (HIV/AIDS is a major problem, followed by cholera), and drought, with less incidence of damaging winds, fires, and insect infestations. These disasters often are widespread and cause critical problems for nations for months or even years at a time. By creating severe economic hardships and endangering health, disasters contribute to long-term problems of poverty, food security, labor migration, and degradation of the environment.

When floods, droughts, or earthquakes come, they often destroy the basics of daily life that women are expected to provide for their families. Recurring or prolonged disasters further increase the vulnerability of women, as men may give up on making a living where their families are located and seek stable jobs elsewhere. And when natural disasters create financial desperation, it is often the women who pay the price through the sale of their few personal belonging or through the forced marriages of their daughters. The following is a look at some ways in which natural disasters affect women's lives.

Decline in Food and Income, and Challenges to Health

Since 80% of Africa's farmers are women, the food shortages created by floods or prolonged droughts create serious hardships for women.[4] The flooding of the Umgeni River in KwaZulu-Natal in South Africa affected women more than men, as social norms hold women responsible for feeding their families.[5] Yet the crop failures not only affected the food that women are growing to feed their families from day to day. When crops are destroyed, women no longer have surplus food to sell, which means they can't generate income to pay for the food items they can't grow (such as salt, oil, or tea), clothing, school fees, or medical care.

When shortages of food are severe over time, people become ill and may die. The very old, the very young (mothers' milk dries up when they don't have sufficient food), people with debilitating diseases, and females in general have the highest mortality rates. Observers describe the suffering in villages in Zambia and Swaziland during the third year of a drought:

Table 1: Natural Disasters in Southern Africa 1981-2008

Country	No. of Events	Drought	Flood	Wild-fire/ storm	Earthquake & Tsunami	Epidemic	Insect Infestation	Pop. Density 2008	Average # people affected per year	Pop. 2008
Angola	39	6	18			15		10.1	121,314	12,531,000
Botswana	10	3	4			2	1	3.1	53,417	1,842,000
Lesotho	15	4	3	6		2		70.1	76,806	2,128,000
Mozambique	65	9	18	16	1	20	1	26.6	765,607	21,285,000
Namibia	19	6	8			5		2.5	32,776	2,089,000
South Africa	67	7	23	25	6	6		35.9	635,179	43,786,000
Swaziland	14	5	2	4		3		65.0	98,072	1,123,605
Zimbabwe	29	5	6	2		16		31.7	544,734	12,383,000
Zambia	32	5	11			15	1	15.5	335,381	11,670,000
TOTAL	**290**	**50**	**93**	**53**	**7**	**84**	**3**	**6.4**	**2,663,286**	**108,837,605**

Source: Country Disaster Statistics. *PreventionWeb: Serving the information needs of the disaster reduction community*. From www.preventionweb.net/english/countries/ statistics . Retrieved June 6, 2009. Area and population data from World Statistics by population (2008), *Tropical Rainforest Conservation* www.mongabay.com/igapo/ world_statistics_by_pop and the *CIA World Factbook*, www.cia.gov/library/publications/the-world-factbook.

Food is scarce, and people, especially old women, are starving. They are very thin and suffer badly from diseases such as dysentery, diarrhea, and scabies, skipping meals in order to feed their children.[6]

…many families have not had a meal in weeks. They depend on roots, wild fruit, and even dead game meat. The old, especially women, have not been leaving huts due to weakness caused by hunger. They lay in their huts, waiting for death.[7]

Increased Workload

Cattle are a major source of food and income in Southern Africa and serve as reserves of wealth (as with savings in the bank, cattle can be turned into cash as needed). During a drought, pastures dry up and cattle begin to weaken and die without food or water. In floods, cattle often drown or become injured. Since they are used for plowing and harvesting, there is a reduction of draught power when cattle die, and women become the tillers and transport. Eventually less land can be cultivated, and women's health often suffers from the combination of diminishing food and overwork.[8]

In Southern Africa, it is women and children who collect water and fuel for the family's needs. During prolonged droughts, women walk much longer distances in search of water, wild fruits, and firewood for cooking. Women hold their families together by providing daily subsistence and will give up their share of food to save members of their families. Observers have noted that:

Women walk for two to three hours in search of water. In villages with open wells, they sometimes do not have the tins and ropes to get the water out of the wells, which means a further walk of about an hour to borrow a rope and a tin, draw water, and then return the rope.[9] … In another village in the Petauke District women had to wake up as early as 4:00 am to walk for at least 10 kilometers to neighboring villages to search for water. In Swaziland, women were seen making daily pilgrimages of approximately 15 miles to the few remaining water sources, with large containers balanced on their heads.[10]

In an effort to restore the family's economic viability, many men leave their families to find work in more economically prosperous places and send money back home. There is a long tradition in Southern Africa of men (and some women) leaving rural communities to work in the mining industries or large farms of South Africa. Such men often live in hostels run by their employers and return home once or twice a year. When husbands leave to find work elsewhere, women's lives become even more difficult, as they must take on the work and responsibilities normally handled by their husbands. When recurrent natural disasters have led to increased male labor migration, family structures may eventually break down:

In some cases, the trappings of city/town life have turned the otherwise seasonal migrant workers into permanent urban dwellers, with a second wife or more in their second homes. A husband in town may even require his wife in the rural areas to send food to him and his other wife after the harvest, and this practice increases in drought periods.[11]

These situations—loss of work animals; the daily search for water, food, and fuel; and husbands leaving to work in other cities or nations—create major hardships for women as they try to maintain their households.

Forced Marriages and Rape

During natural disasters, families sometimes become desperate due to lack of food, shelter, and basic resources. In order to raise enough money for the family to survive, the family (usually the father or grandfather) may force a daughter to marry. In many Southern African societies, the husband's family gives the bride's family gifts of money or goods, which are called *lobola*.[12] A forced marriage in effect uses a daughter as a disposable resource to raise money to sustain the other family members. Forced marriages not only make young girls marry someone they did not choose; they also affect other women, because wives of wealthy men may suddenly find themselves in polygamous marriages. Multiple sexual partners have negative health implications, as they may lead to the escalation of sexually transmitted diseases and exacerbate the spread of HIV/AIDS, which is a major health problem across nations in Southern Africa.

Rape and sexual violence increase in the wake of disasters. Women are more likely to be targeted for such violence, and their physical and mental suffering can continue long after such acts, as they are unlikely to get appropriate health care. If pregnant, they may lose the baby due to the violence to which they are subjected and may contract HIV/AIDS from the rapists. Afterwards, women may be blamed for "allowing" themselves to be raped, and then be ostracized or shunned by their husbands or other family members.[13]

Instructional and Classroom Applications

Students need to listen to women to understand the issues facing them when disasters strike. Some websites allow students to listen as women across the world describe their situations and actions. Here are some good online sources for such study:

The United Nations Development Programme website at www.undp.org/cpr/we_do/integrating_risk.shtml has numerous videos that can be used at the high-school level to learn about many facets of the challenges women face. Also see the section on "Voices from Countries in Crisis" for case studies.

The International Museum of Women has an online show entitled "Women, Power and Politics" that also provides material for case studies from six world regions to hear about women's issues and their actions. Here are two examples from the 35 cases:

Women, Natural Disasters, and Reconstruction
(www.imow.org/wpp/stories/viewStory?storyId=1383)
Women Thrive Worldwide, a nonprofit organization that advocates for U.S. foreign policy to foster economic opportunities for women, remembers the cyclones in Myanmar/Burma and the disproportionate impact that natural disasters have on women and children's lives.

Congo: Stop Sexual Violence
(www.imow.org/wpp/stories/viewStory?storyId=1082)
The Global Fund for Women calls for the international community to take action to put an end to the epidemic of rape and sexual aggression in the Democratic Republic of Congo.

Other primary sources that explicate women's issues can be found at the United Nations Population Fund at unfpa.org/public.

Look through these sites and review the videos and text. Either make selections for the students or have them select from ones you find appropriate. Have students listen and present the views and experiences of these women, then look for commonalities across different world regions. As a follow up, they can make connections with women's issues in their own community or country.

Marginalized by Aid

Private voluntary aid organizations and governments often respond to disasters by offering programs in which people can work for food or cash to help them survive while recovery and rebuilding is taking place. Since most aid programs are devised by men and target male heads of households, women's situations may not be considered in the planning or execution. Many households desperate for food or money do not have an adult who is able to leave the family and work eight or more hours a day to receive aid. Mothers have to take care of infants or young children, and elderly grandmothers (who are often heads of families where AIDS has sickened or killed the mother and father) may not be physically able to carry out the required labor.[14]

Women's limited access to government programs or private voluntary organizations is symptomatic of larger issues of the barriers women face in owning land, inheriting wealth, and the inability to control their own lives. The following is an excerpt of stories from *Zimbabwe Women's Voices* that demonstrates the contexts faced by rural women regarding the land tenure system and patriarchal control:

> Things went wrong this year in June when my husband died. One of his sons, who was married and stayed with his family nearby took for himself the land left by his father and put it in his name. So I have no land left. My husband's relatives had suggested I become my husband's cousin's new wife. But he refused. I am now staying all alone in poverty, since my husband's brother could not take me as a wife, having one of his own.[15]

Traditionally in Botswana, all property goes to male heirs, so that upon the death of a husband or father, the home, cattle-post (ranch), or land is inherited by close male relatives who then have the right to decide what, if anything, to give his sisters, wife, or mother. Women have to work through male relatives in order to negotiate with banks and other institutions that subordinate and render them as dependents to their fathers, husbands, brothers, and sons.

This exclusion from decision-making processes puts women at high risk of losing income or wealth as they can't partake in decisions involving their own lives, build businesses on their own, or control money that they earn. Their social roles as care-givers are sometimes referred to as "invisible earnings" due to lack of recognition for their contributions. Gender roles exacerbate their vulnerability, in that they limit women's mobility and opportunities for political involvement, education, access to information, and markets. Women are more vulnerable than men, not because it is in their nature to be weak, but because of restrictive patrilineal norms that result in impoverishment, political marginalization, and dependence on men.[16]

Women Respond

Women in Southern Africa are often portrayed as helpless and passive victims of natural disasters, with images shown on American media of starvation, disease, or violence. The news rarely mentions how women are able to take action to care for their families and rebuild their lives. When learning about women living in poverty, it's critical that students spend as much time focusing on how the women develop coping strategies, take action to deal with problems, and improve their situations, as it is to study the hardships they endure. Students need to appreciate the women's strength, creativity, and perseverance, as well as the cooperative networks they develop to ensure basic human needs of food, shelter, income, and security.

Alternative Foodstuffs

In previous generations when crops were wiped out because of drought or floods, women might seek out wild food sources for home consumption and sale. One of the traditional foods sought during droughts were mophani caterpillars, the first stage of the Emperor Moth that only eats the leaves of the mophani tree. These caterpillars are collected, cooked, and dried, then used in stews along with vegetables.

In some places, they were sold as crunchy snacks (described by some as being similar to popcorn), and in recent years, they have been packaged for sale in markets. In South Africa, the harvesting of caterpillars has grown into a commercial business with multinational food companies now selling the processed caterpillars in supermarkets in the United Kingdom and on the Internet.[17] Women are now not only harvesting caterpillars as a supplementary source of protein, but they have found a new source of income. As a result, these caterpillars are threatened with extinction. Women sometimes cut mophani trees down to use as fuel, which complicates the destruction brought by other natural disasters.[18]

Networking and Organizing

From time immemorial, women in Southern Africa have been known for their self-aid through social networking groups. In Botswana, Zimbabwe, and South Africa, women have found success by creating rotating savings associations, called "rounds" or (depending on the ethnic group) known as *motshelo, stokvels,*

or *mahodisanas*. Membership varies widely but is usually relatively small, ranging from five to twenty-five. In these informal, voluntary savings associations, women meet at a regular time to contribute an agreed-upon amount of money. The money collected may be given to a member on a rotating basis (so each member has a turn within a few weeks) or the meetings may be used to discuss special requests from members to receive small loans from the communal monies. In this way, when a women has a hardship (her crop fails) or a family obligation (a relative marries), she can access ready cash. There are thousands of such groups across Africa.[19]

There are many other groups that are empowering women though economic and political organizing. Women in Business (WIB) was established in Zimbabwe to support women's enterprises by helping them expand their businesses and deal with government regulations. The Zimbabwe Women's Finance Trust grants loans to low income entrepreneurs who are setting up small businesses such as knitting, selling eggs or poultry, or brickmaking. Others include the Women's Resource Center and the Musasa Project Trust.

Zambian women have formed clubs to address the tragedies that come with extended drought. Nawina Hamaundu writes of women organizing: "Women like Tendani Bandawa who, with six children and a husband who had just run away, could stand up in a crowd of over one thousand people and announce that she would like to be fully involved in her village's development."[20] Women demonstrate a determination to persevere and make a difference.

Kinship Alliance

African societies highly value the kinship of large, multigenerational, extended families that are characterized by complex systems of obligations. In many societies in Southern Africa, a man is obligated to care for the widow of his brother or educate the children of needy relatives. Although such obligations have changed somewhat with the effects of urbanization and HIV/AIDS, women often first turn to their relatives to secure safe shelter and meet basic needs, both financial and emotional. However, family ties can also contribute to stress following natural disasters when women are expected to take care of additional family members or share what little they have with their husband's family.[21]

Sacrifice

Often it is women and girls who make sacrifices to support the family in times of disaster. In a crisis, women's sole assets such as jewelry or small livestock are often the first to be sold to provide for basic needs. Men's assets (such as land, large animals, or machines) are held as long as possible, in part because they are considered more important and harder to replace once the crisis is over. Natural disasters may lead families with few resources to pull children out of school as their labor is needed to make money. In most countries, girls' school attendance is affected more than that of boys. The impact of constraining girls' education hurts women's reproductive health, earning power, and the health of future children. In cases of lack of food in extreme need, women may become "shock absorbers" by reducing their own food consumption to keep children or elders alive.[22]

Conclusion

What can be done to change the economic, social, and health risks of women and girls during and after natural disasters in Southern Africa? Raising the status of women through education, changes in laws of inheritance, and microfinance are some first steps. Women need to be decision-makers to incorporate women's issues, knowledge, and perspectives into the planning and implementation of development and disaster prevention programs. Management for natural disasters that relies on women's needs and experiences is much more likely to reduce the family issues discussed above, as women will work towards ensuring security against violence and access to food and water, and promote ways to keep families together. Women's priorities are essential to protect the heart of society—the family. 🖎

NOTES

1. See the following websites: African Commission on Human and Peoples' Rights, www.achpr.org/english/_info/news_en.html; Special Rapporteur on the Rights of Women, www.achpr.org/english/_info/women_prot.htm.

2. The World Revolution: The State of the World, www.worldrevolution.org/projects/globalissuesoverview/overview2/BriefOverview.htm.

3. Elaine Enarson, "Gender and Natural Disasters." (International Labour Organization, Geneva, Switzerland, 2000). www.ilo.org/public/english/employment/crisis/download/criswp1.pdf.

4. Wilfred Tichagwa, "The Effects of Drought on the Condition of Women," *Gender and Development* 2, no.1 (1994): 20-25; Astrid Von Kotze, "Why Women Are a Gender Issue," *Agenda*, no.29; *Women and the Environment* (1996): 22-26.

5. Von Kotze.

6. Nawina Hamaundu, "Women in the Eastern Province: More Hit by Drought and Yet More Enduring." *Gender and Development* 1, no.1 (1993): 41-44.

7. *Ibid.*

8. Tichagwa.

9. Hamaundu, 41.

10. John Wright and Helen Ford, "Letter from Africa: Another African Disaster" *Bio-Medical Journal* 305 (1992): 1479-1480.

11. Tichagwa, 23.

12. *Ibid.* Lobola traditionally was a gift of cattle (since cattle were the primary source of wealth in most societies with this custom) to acknowledge the money and time the family had invested in raising a good woman who would, in turn, be a good wife. In contemporary societies, people have turned to cash payments. The process of paying lobola is quite long and complex as it involves many members of both the bride and groom's extended families. The amounts asked are usually discussed and negotiated upon before the two families reach a consensus. For voices of women speaking about lobola, see "From Fiona: Lobola... Ready to be Sold?" By Fiona Abassa: May 1, 2007 at www.ugpulse.com/articles/daily/homepage.asp?ID=611. Also see "Lobola....the day the bride price is paid" about lobola today in a wedding announcement, December 2, 2008, at www.wellsphere.com/hiv-aids-article/lobola-hellip-the-day-the-bride-price-is-paid/518141

13. World Health Organization, *World Report on Violence and Health* (Geneva, Switzerland: World Health Organization, 2002).

14. Tichagwa.

15. Mary Johnson Osirim, "Making Good on Commitments to Grassroots Women: NGOs and Empowerment in Contemporary Zimbabwe," *Women's Studies International Forum* 24, no.2 (2001): 167-180.

16. Mary B. Anderson, "Understanding the Disaster-Development Continuum: Gender Analysis is the Essential Tool," *Gender & Development* 12, no.1 (February 1994): 7-10.

17. Tichagwa.

18. Von Kotze; Tichagwa. For an advertisement of the caterpillars as snack food, see www.stylehive.com/bookmark/edible-mopani-worms-333758.

19. Osirim. For more data see www.fao.org/docrep/005/y4094E/y4094e04.htm and eh.net/XIIICongress/Papers/Verhoef.pdf .

20. Hamaundu, 42.

21. Yaw Oheneba-Sakyi and Baffour K. Takyi, Eds. *African Families at the Turn of the 21st Century.* (Westport, CT: Praeger Publishers, 2006).

22. Agnes Quisumbing, Ruth Meinzen-Dick, and Lucy Bassett with contributions by Michael Usnick, Lauren Pandolfelli, Cheryl Morden, and Harold Alderman, *Policy Brief No. 007: Helping Women Respond to the Global Food Price Crisis* (International Food Policy Research Institute, 2006). Available at www.ifpri.org/PUBS/bp/bp007.asp.

CHAPTER 10

MUHAMMAD YUNUS AND THE GRAMEEN BANK: "BEING POOR DOESN'T MAKE YOU POOR QUALITY"

VALERIE OOKA PANG

NATURAL DISASTERS ARE CONTINUAL THREATS around the world. Whether the disaster is due to a tsunami or an earthquake, people with little money are most at risk because they find themselves unable to rebuild or make a living once a disaster has struck. One individual, Muhammad Yunus, believes in the resilience and hard work of the poorest people, those with an income equivalent to a dollar per day or less. He creatively addresses a key human issue of poverty, one that has been exacerbated by a string of natural disasters in his native country of Bangladesh.[1]

Bangladeshis have suffered from a series of natural disasters; most are cyclones that have been identified as some of the most destructive disasters in the world. For example, in 1942, 1961, 1963, and 1965, deadly cyclones struck the country. In the past forty years, the two most damaging tropical cyclones hit the country in 1970 and 1991. The largest loss of lives occurred in 1991, when 140,000 people died.[2] These disasters brought severe drought and famine. Later, a severe flood hit the country in 1998, due to continuous monsoons. Flooding is an ongoing problem because much of Bangladesh is located in low-lying lands. In addition, Bangladesh is one of the most densely populated nations in the world, with 2,639 people per square mile, so when a disaster hits, countless people are affected. After a natural disaster, many people find themselves unable to sustain themselves and their families.

Muhammad Yunus, an economist, could not understand why honored economic theories did not work to solve the financial and survival needs of Bangladeshis. After constant crises brought on or magnified by natural disasters, people were continually starving. Yunus found that many farmers could grow crops and feed themselves, but city dwellers had very limited ways to subsist. Though they lacked material wealth, he determined that the individuals who were labeled "poor" were not poor in spirit. The people were independent and strong minded; they

deserved support and protection for their human rights. Yunus's beliefs were analogous to the Universal Declaration of Human Rights, which states that "recognition of the inherent dignity and of the equal and inalienable rights of all members of the human family is the foundation of freedom, justice and peace in the world."[3] He wanted all people, no matter how poor, to have the opportunity to create a life of dignity and worth, where they are able to exercise their rights—such as the right to work, the right to an education, the right to own property, and the right to family life. The research Yunus conducted in his local community led him to understand more fully the needs of his fellow humans and resulted in his creation of the Grameen Bank. This bank became the self-empowerment vehicle for millions of members who benefited from the concept of microcredit.

Natural Disasters, Human Rights, and Poverty

The two most destructive natural disasters to strike Bangladesh in recent times were a cyclone and a flood. The massive cyclone of 1970 resulted in drought and famine that significantly increased the numbers living in poverty. And in 1998, "THE FLOOD," as Yunus called it, covered a majority of the country for eleven weeks, forcing 30 million people from their homes.[4] Thousands lost their homes, businesses, and other buildings; they were left without food, water, shelter, medicine, and schools. Though natural disasters created difficult conditions for Bangladeshis, Yunus wrote:

> [W]idespread poverty...is a man-made phenomenon. Cyclones, floods, and tidal surges occur in other countries. In most, they do not cause human misery of the magnitude we see in Bangladesh. The reason is that, in these countries, the people are rich enough to build protective systems and strong embankments. Furthermore, poverty and overcrowding have pushed

the countless poor in Bangladesh to seek their livelihoods in more and more unsafe areas of the country... Thus, poverty doesn't only condemn humans to lives of difficulty and unhappiness...poverty denies people any semblance of control over their destiny, it is the ultimate denial of human rights.[5]

Yunus also stated, "Poverty is the absence of all human rights."[6]

In 2006, the Norwegian Nobel Committee awarded Yunus and the Grameen Bank the Nobel Peace Prize, because the committee believed that the advancement of human rights and democracy can be achieved by addressing poverty. In his Nobel Lecture, representing the Grameen Bank and himself, Yunus clearly identified economic and political structures and belief systems that create the underclass:

> Poverty is created because we built our theoretical framework on assumptions which under-estimate human capacity, by designing concepts which are too narrow (such as concepts of business, credit-worthiness, entrepreneurship, employment) or developing institutions, which remain half-done (such as financial institutions, where poor are left out). Poverty is caused by the failure at the conceptual level, rather than any lack of capability on the part of people.[7]

Yunus believed the people in Bangladesh, especially the poorest individuals, had the determination and will to develop successful businesses; they simply needed credit to do so.

Yunus believes in human rights for all and is a strong supporter of self-empowerment. He left a faculty position at Middle Tennessee State University in 1972 to support the independence movement of Bangladesh. The area had been designated as part of Pakistan since 1947 when the British Parliament withdrew their control and established the Indian Union and the separate, independent state of Pakistan. Political unrest, along with natural disasters of cyclones, flooding, and drought, had crippled the country and poverty was widespread.[8]

Capitalism and the Beginnings of the Grameen Bank

When Yunus returned to Bangladesh in 1972, Chittagong University hired him as a professor of economics. He studied the financial system of the area near the university. He questioned the economic theories he had studied; they were not working. He believed that despite natural disasters and political instability, there should be ways for people to support their basic needs

Curriculum Implications: Creating an Issues-centered Unit

This chapter provides background information about how one person, Muhammad Yunus, developed the economic concept of microcredit and built an organization, the Grameen Bank, to fight poverty that was exacerbated by natural disasters. An issues-centered unit on the intersection of natural disasters, human rights, and microcredit for middle and high school students should be taught in social studies classes.[9] In addition, students should reflect upon and discuss one of Yunus's essential beliefs, "Being poor doesn't make you poor quality."[10]

Social Studies Standards
❼ PRODUCTION, DISTRIBUTION, AND CONSUMPTION
Explain and demonstrate the role of money in everyday life.

❾ GLOBAL CONNECTIONS
Challenge learners to analyze the causes, consequences, and possible solutions to persistent, contemporary, and emerging global issues such as health care, security, resource allocation, economic development, and environmental quality.

Several focal questions can be used to shape an issues-centered unit on human rights and the poverty created by natural disasters:

- ▶ Why do we have poor people? What makes them poor?
- ▶ Who is responsible for addressing the issue of poverty?
- ▶ What conditions create poverty?
- ▶ Should credit be considered a human right? Why or why not?
- ▶ How effective has microcredit been in eradicating poverty in Bangladesh and around the globe?
- ▶ What roles has the Grameen Bank played in eradicating poverty?
- ▶ Should other countries create the same type of microfinance model in their country? Why or why not?
- ▶ How effective would microcredit be with the poor in the United States?

The teacher can also place students in discussion groups so they can collaboratively arrive at focal questions. They may want to pick several from those listed above or create others to be used to guide their unit.

Extending Learning: Student Involvement in Eradicating Global Poverty[11]

Once students have developed a basic understanding of microcredit and the cycle of extreme poverty that plagues families around the world from natural disasters, teachers can facilitate a service-learning project in which students become actively involved in financing an entrepreneur who has been the victim of a cyclone, earthquake, tsunami, or other disaster.

Working in collaborative groups, students can access specific information about individuals or groups seeking business loans through websites such as www.kiva.org. Kiva, whose slogan is "loans that change lives," has a website that offers a simple, easy way to navigate through the site. By searching on this and similar sites for individuals who are rebuilding their lives after a disaster, students can learn background information about the local community and persons seeking the loan; identify risks; understand how their money will be used to expand, supply, or create the business; and develop an avenue by which recipients can send updates about their progress. Students can also see how families and communities have been affected in life-changing ways by the loans they've financed.

Before providing funds for a victim of a natural disaster, students can persuade businesses and other people that their choice is a worthy cause with a low risk of default. For example, Kiva's website profiles Punahou School in Honolulu, Hawaii, which has lent almost $33,000 to small businesses through its senior capstone course, "Social Entrepreneurship, Economics, and Deeds of Service," and has made microcredit an integral strategy of its coursework.

Microcredit for victims of natural disasters as a service-learning project encourages students to become active participants in solutions to real-world problems. Students learn that they have the potential to change lives and support the protection of human rights.

Important Quotes from Yunus: Discussion Starters

Students benefit from dialogue with others about the issues raised in this chapter. The following quotes provide discussion starters for teachers to use in their classrooms:

> Generous assistance from people within the country and around the world has saved tens of thousands of lives in Bangladesh after floods and tidal waves. Yet nonprofits alone have proven to be an inadequate response to social problems. The persistence and even worsening of global poverty, endemic disease, homelessness, famine, and pollution are sufficient evidence that charity by itself cannot do the job...Charity is a form of trickle-down economics; if the trickle stops, so does help for the needy.[12]

> Experts on poverty alleviation insist that training is absolutely vital for the poor to move up the economic ladder. But if you go out into the real world, you cannot miss seeing that the poor are poor not because they are untrained or illiterate but because they cannot retain the returns of their labor. They have no control over capital, and it is the ability to control capital that gives people the power to rise out of poverty. Profit is unashamedly biased toward capital. In their powerless state, the poor work for the benefit of someone who controls the productive assets.[13]

**SCHOOL OF EDUCATION
CURRICULUM LABORATORY
UM-DEARBORN**

of food, shelter, and safety. During his research, Yunus talked with a young mother who worked from morning until evening weaving beautiful bamboo stools, yet she only earned two cents for each stool. He discovered that she was borrowing nine cents to buy raw materials, and after repaying the moneylender and selling the stools back to him, she only had two cents left. Due to the high interest rates being charged and the inability to sell the stools on her own, the mother could not make any profit.[14] Yunus believed in the free-market system; he believed that hardworking people who utilized capitalistic tools should be able to pull themselves out of poverty. In a study of the community, Yunus and his graduate students discovered a group of 43 people who owed the moneylenders a total of $27. Their lives were being shackled by these loans; the cycle of poverty could not be broken because the people could not get credit. Yunus personally lent $27 to the 43 people so they could pay off the moneylenders. This was the beginning of his use of microcredit and the beginning of the Grameen Bank, a bank that provides seed funds for small businesses.

Yunus believes in capitalism as a system that supports a society where the dignity and rights of all are respected, not as a system for maximum profit and runaway greed. He wrote: "Capitalism takes a narrow view of human nature, assuming that people are one-dimensional beings concerned only with the pursuit of maximum profit... Mainstream free-market theory suffers from a 'conceptualization failure,' a failure to capture what it is to be human... People are not one-dimensional entities; they are excitingly multi-dimensional."[15] Although Yunus thought people must give up some personal freedom in order to "enhance our own security, safety, and long-term happiness,"[16] he believed that it was possible to utilize capitalism so that people had opportunities to sustain themselves, and build communities and nations for the long term.[17]

Economic Beliefs Underlying the Grameen Bank

The Grameen Bank is built upon Yunus's economic beliefs. He believed that banks should loan money to the poorest people in society because they had the most need. However, banks asked for collateral. Yunus did not believe his borrowers should provide collateral because he knew that the poor did not have resources to place as guarantees. From his novel perspective, he saw credit as a human right, because he believed credit to be the key to the ability of individuals to participate in a capitalist system.[18] Credit provides opportunities.

The word *grameen* means "rural" or "village" in the Bengali language. Grameen Bank gives out small loans to individuals

who create a small venture, and from the profits, entrepreneurs are able to slowly move out of poverty. In the early years of the Grameen Bank, one of its initial projects was to organize a farmers' association where a new irrigation system was built, and water was distributed to farms.[19] This allowed for more crops to be grown in extreme drought conditions.

The Grameen Bank is owned by those who have taken out loans; they become members. The bank provides loans to individuals and creates small community groups of 5 members, because through this small unit, strong social bonds develop.[20] The members of the Bank found that this configuration worked more effectively than cooperatives of 30 or more people. Members of small groups were more engaged in bank activities than when they were part of larger cooperatives. When members repay their loans, the small group decides who deserves credit next in the community. In this way, loans become self-sustaining. Most individuals who have taken out loans from Grameen Bank are women, and these entrepreneurial women have had a major impact on the success of families leaving poverty.[21]

Yunus and the Grameen Bank have faced various challenges. For example, members of the Bank, like most people in Bangladesh, had to cope with the consequences of THE FLOOD of 1998. A majority of the country was under water, and about 70% of the members of the Bank were affected.[22] Many members were not able to continue paying back their loans. During this crisis, the Grameen Bank loaned out additional funds to members so they could fix their homes; most loans were about $125. The Bank also established a new policy that encouraged members to set up a disaster fund. One of the core values of the Grameen Bank is that "handouts" or charity are not productive because they do not build self-empowerment in people. So the members, who received wheat to grow after THE FLOOD from Grameen Bank, deposited funds into a community disaster fund that could be used after future disasters.

The work of Yunus and the Grameen Bank continues to evolve. Yunus has created a new concept called *social business*, which refers to a business that is "cause driven rather than profit driven."[23] One of their first social business projects is Grameen Danone, owned by the Grameen Bank in cooperation with the Danone Yogurt company. The facility produces enriched yogurt that is inexpensive enough that poor people can buy it for their families. In addition, the product is made and sold by members of the Grameen Bank. Yunus has defined a social business as one that is self-sustaining. Original investors get back their investment, however, they do not receive any profits. The earned income is placed back into the company or another company that is designed to support the community.[24] The Grameen Bank is adding this new direction to its work—an example of how capitalism is being utilized to build stable businesses that can withstand the effects of a natural disaster.

The Grameen Bank: A Way of Thinking

Yunus built the Grameen Bank, which now has approximately 7.5 million owners, 97% of whom are women.[25] Approximately 6.5 billon dollars has been loaned since the Bank began in 1976, and the loan repayment rate is 98.6%.[26] Yunus's principles and Grameen Bank methods have been utilized all over the world—there are microcredit programs in the Philippines, India, Arkansas, and Illinois. Yunus has also expanded microcredit to providing the poor with loans for homes and education. Though the term *microcredit* or *microfinancing* is utilized by a variety of individuals and organizations, Yunus and members of the Grameen Bank have identified a way of thinking about the Grameen Bank that includes the following (Grameen Bank website):

> *It promotes credit as a human right*
> Its mission is to help the poor families to help themselves to overcome poverty. It is targeted to the poor, particularly poor women.
> [The] most distinctive feature of Grameen credit is that it is not based on any collateral, or legally enforceable contracts. It is based on "trust," not on legal procedures and systems.
> It is offered for creating self-employment for income-generating activities and housing for the poor, as opposed to consumption.

The development and use of microcredit has been an influential practice that is providing opportunities to millions of people throughout the world.

Conclusion

Cyclones, continuing monsoons, floods, and famine are among the disasters that have devastated Bangladesh for many years. Muhammad Yunus searched for an economic model and practice to address severe poverty, a common result of disasters. He saw the potential in poor people; he saw their spirit. As Yunus said, "Being poor doesn't make you poor quality." From this deep conviction, he developed a microcredit system that has been employed throughout the world, and a view that credit is a human right. He has proven that poor people, even the poorest, are safe financial risks, and they work hard to move out of poverty when provided resources. Initially, numerous small loans of about $30 to $50 from the Grameen Bank financed the development of millions of new businesses, mostly owned by women. Presently, loans range from $100-$300. Yunus's work and the efforts of Grameen Bank members have transformed the way others think about the potential of the poor and the role of credit in eradicating helplessness and poverty.

NOTES

1. Muhammad Yunus and Karl Weber, *Creating a World Without Poverty: Social Business and the Future of Capitalism* (New York: Public Affairs, 2007), p. 19.

2. Bryan Walsh, Top 10 Natural Disasters, *Time Magazine*, Accessed on August 31, 2009. www.time.com/time/specials/2007/top10/article/0,30583,1686204_1686252_1690260,00.html.

3. United Nations, 1948, Universal Declaration of Human Rights. Accessed on October 20, 2007. www.un.org/Overview/rights.html.

4. Yunus and Weber.

5. *Ibid.*, p. 104.

6. Muhammad Yunus, Nobel Lecture Given By Nobel Peace Prize Laureate, Oslo, Sweden (December 10, 2006). nobelprize.org/nobel_prizes/peace/laureates/2006/yunus-lecture-en.html.

7. *Ibid.*

8. Muhammad Yunus, *Banker to the Poor: Microlending and the Battle against World Poverty* (New York: Public Affairs, 2003).

9. Valerie Ooka Pang and Karl Grobl, *Microfinancing and Human Rights*, Presentation at the annual meeting of the National Council for the Social Studies, November 2007, in San Diego, California; Michelle Yvonne Szpara, Iftikhar Ahmad, and Patricia Velde Pederson, "Nobel Peace Laureate Muhammad Yunus: A Banker Who Believes Credit Is a Human Right," *Social Education* 71, no. 1 (2007): 9-14.

10. Muhammad Yunus, *Social Enterprise: Doing Well by Doing Good*, presentation at the University of California, San Diego, October 21, 2007.

11. These ideas were contributed by Tamiko Stratton, a teacher at Kearny High School in San Diego City Schools. I would also like to acknowledge the contributions of Margaret Fairfield.

12. Yunus and Weber, p. 6.

13. Yunus, 2003, p. 141.

14. See Yunus, 2003, *op. cit.*

15. Yunus and Weber, p. 18.

16. *Ibid.*, p. 212.

17. Yunus, 2003.

18. *Ibid.*, p. 103.

19. Yunus and Weber, p. 45.

20. Count, p. 70.

21. Yunus and Weber, 2006; Yunus, 2003.

22. Yunus and Weber, p. 61.

23. *Ibid*, p. 22.

24. *Ibid.*

25. *Ibid.*

26. *Ibid.*, p. 51.

PART 3
SECURING THE HUMAN RIGHTS OF VICTIMS

CHAPTER 11

PROTECTING HUMAN RIGHTS AFTER NATURAL DISASTERS

WALTER KÄLIN

ON JULY 27, 2006, the United Nations Human Rights Committee raised concerns about "information that the poor, and in particular African-Americans, were disadvantaged by the rescue and evacuation plans implemented when Hurricane Katrina hit the United States, and continue to be disadvantaged under the reconstruction plans." It recommended that the U.S. "review its practices and policies to ensure the full implementation of its obligation to protect life and of the prohibition of discrimination…in matters related to disaster prevention and preparedness, emergency assistance and relief measures."[1] Thus, the Committee was concerned that U.S. policies in the aftermath of Hurricane Katrina contradicted international human rights guarantees protecting life and prohibiting discrimination. Other United Nations human rights bodies raised similar concerns.[2]

This was not U.S. bashing, singling out a particular country for criticism. Rather, human rights concerns were also raised in the context of other mega-disasters. In the aftermath of the 2004 Indian Ocean Tsunami, the Representative of the U.N. Secretary General on the Human Rights of Internally Displaced Persons stated that "in the understandable rush to provide assistance to the survivors of the Tsunami, insufficient attention has been devoted to protecting the human rights of those forcibly displaced by the disaster," in particular, regarding discrimination in aid provision, enforced relocation, sexual and gender-based violence, recruitment of children into fighting forces, and the difficulties of rightful owners in having their land restituted to them.[3] When the 2005 earthquake in the Himalayas triggered a large-scale humanitarian operation in Pakistan, the Office of the High Commissioner for Human Rights for the first time sent a human rights advisor to a country hit by a natural disaster.

Why Human Rights?

Human rights violations are usually associated with armed conflict or authoritarian regimes but not natural disasters. However, human rights activists and the humanitarian community are increasingly finding that persons affected by floods, earthquakes, hurricanes, volcano eruptions, and other disasters may face multiple human rights challenges in the aftermath of such disastrous events. Natural disasters often force people to flee danger zones, and such displacement creates particular vulnerabilities. Being displaced means that from one day to the next people lose their homes, property, and livelihoods; are forced to leave behind all they cherish; and risk ending up in marginalization, poverty, and exploitation. In short, displacement shatters lives and communities. But even where people are not displaced in the aftermath of natural disasters, pre-existing patterns of discrimination and other human rights violations are often exacerbated, putting the already marginalized and vulnerable people at an increased risk of human rights abuses.

The result can be insufficient or inappropriate protection from continuing threats caused by the effects of the disaster; unequal access to humanitarian assistance, in particular for displaced women; discrimination in the provision of assistance; sexual- and gender-based violence, particularly in collective shelters or camps; infringements of the right to education (e.g., when schools are used as shelters for a prolonged period of time); non-replacement of lost, confiscated, or destroyed documentation; economic and sexual exploitation of children in the absence of sufficient assistance; unsafe or involuntary returns or forced relocations to other parts of the country; or failure to restitute property and reconstruct houses or ensure compensation.

Such disregard for the human rights of those affected by natural disasters is not necessarily intentional, but often results from inappropriate policies, a lack of capacity to appropriately respond to the disaster and the challenges of reconstruction, or simple neglect or oversight.

Recognizing the human rights challenges associated with natural disasters is particularly important in light of climate change and the likelihood associated with it of an increase, in the coming years and decades, of hurricanes and floods as well as slow-onset disasters such as droughts and environmental degradation caused by rising sea-levels. It is believed that due to the effects of climate change, 50- 250 million people may move by the middle of the century, either within their countries or across borders, on a permanent or temporary basis.[4] While some of these movements will be part of a strategy by communities, families, and individuals to adapt to the effects of changing climate (i.e., voluntary and triggered by the prospect of finding a better life in areas not negatively affected), many will be forced to leave their homes as a result of sudden-onset hydro-meteorological disasters or slow-onset environmental degradation.

Human Rights Obligations

Human rights can be understood as the entitlements of individuals (the right-holders) against the State and its authorities (the duty-bearers), during times of peace as well as armed conflict. Human rights are guaranteed by international law to protect the most fundamental human needs.[5] At the international level, it was only in 1948 that governments were ready to recognize the universal character of human rights when, on December 10, 1948, the General Assembly of the United Nations solemnly proclaimed the Universal Declaration of Human Rights. On the basis of that document, a series of binding human rights conventions were negotiated during the subsequent decades. Many of these are relevant for protecting people affected by natural disasters, including the 1966 International Covenant on Civil and Political Rights; the 1966 International Covenant on Economic, Social and Cultural Rights; and the 1989 Convention on the Rights of the Child.[6]

Most human rights guarantees impose multiple obligations on states and their authorities.[7] First, human rights impose a *duty to respect* the right concerned—an obligation to remain passive and refrain from actively infringing with its exercise by the right holder (e.g., not to kill the right holders or to punish them for their political opinions) unless the right in question allows for certain limitations. Second, they impose a *duty to protect*, or an obligation to take active measures if a person, group, or situation threatens the exercise of the right by the right-holder (e.g., through attempts on the right-holder's life); such duty is violated if authorities do not act although they know of the threat and would have the means to protect the victim. Third, human rights, under certain circumstances and within the limits of available means, generate a *duty to fulfill*—an obligation to create necessary laws and institutions, or to provide right holders with certain goods and services necessary for the enjoyment of a particular right (e.g., educational laws setting up a primary school

accessible for all children, food aid for persons threatened by famine). Experience shows that in the context of natural disasters, the duty to protect becomes particularly relevant.

Protection of Internally Displaced Persons

Victims of natural disasters who have fled their homes or been evacuated but remain within their own country are considered to be internally displaced persons (IDPs). Their human rights are codified in the 1998 United Nations *Guiding Principles on Internal Displacement* (hereinafter Guiding Principles). This important document describes internally displaced persons as persons "who have been forced or obliged to flee or to leave their homes or places of habitual residence, in particular as a result of or in order to avoid the effects of…natural or human-made disasters, and who have not crossed an internationally recognized State border."[8] They are not refugees (i.e.. persons who flee abroad and possess only limited rights as aliens in the country of refuge). Rather, they remain citizens or residents of their own country and continue to be entitled to the full range of guarantees available to the general population, and therefore should not be called "environmental" or "disaster refugees."

The Guiding Principles cover all phases of displacement (i.e., protection from displacement, protection during displacement, and protection during the return and recovery phase). They state, for instance, that forced evacuations in cases of disasters are prohibited "unless the safety and health of those affected require" such measures (Principle 6). Evacuations, if they become necessary, must be carried out in a manner that does not violate "the rights to life, dignity, liberty and security of those affected" (Principle 8). As regards humanitarian aid, displaced persons have, as a minimum, the right to be provided with and have safe access to essential food and potable water, basic shelter and housing, appropriate clothing and essential medical services (Principle 18). After the disaster, the displaced have the right to choose between voluntary return to their former homes, integration to where they have been displaced, or moving to another part of the country (Principle 28).

The Guiding Principles, even though not a binding treaty, gain their authority from the fact that they reflect and are consistent with binding human rights law, and are recognized by states as an "important international framework for the protection of internally displaced persons".[9] Several countries have also integrated them into their domestic law.[10]

Particularly Relevant Human Rights Guarantees

With the exception of the Convention on the Rights of Persons with Disabilities (Article 11),[11] none of the UN human rights conventions explicitly addresses the human rights of persons displaced or otherwise affected by natural disasters. Nevertheless, human rights protect persons regardless of their situation and therefore can also be invoked by such people. The following rights are particularly relevant:[12]

Right to Life and Security of Person. While natural disasters often cause casualties, loss of life could sometimes have been avoided had competent authorities alerted, evacuated, or otherwise protected the victims. In such cases, human neglect kills, not the hazards of nature. This is well illustrated by the 2008 Budayeva judgment of the European Court of Human Rights condemning the Russian Federation for violations of the right to life and obliging it to pay compensation to the surviving family members who had brought a claim under the European Convention of Human Rights.[13] The Court stressed that, in the context of natural disasters, the right to life "lays down a positive obligation on States to take appropriate steps to safeguard the lives of those within their jurisdiction"[14] and found that local authorities had failed to take available measures necessary to protect the inhabitants against the deadly consequences of the mudslides. Thus, a state becomes liable for deaths if they occurred because the authorities neglected their duty to take preventive measures against an impending natural hazard although effective means to mitigate the risk would have been available.

The duty to protect is highly relevant in the context of collective shelters and camps for persons displaced by natural disasters. Especially when overcrowded and badly managed, such places increase the risk for women to become victims of sexual and gender-based violence. In some cases (e.g., in Haiti after the 2008 hurricanes and Honduras after Hurricane Mitch in 1998), criminal gangs attacked or infiltrated collective shelters, resulting in robberies, rapes, and even killings due to a lack of law and order or police protection in these places.

Liberty of Movement and Freedom to Choose One's Place of Residence. The duty to take life-saving measures may entail that people must be evacuated or relocated from danger zones against their will (i.e., forcibly displaced) as long as their safety would be at risk. Particularly in Latin America and Asia, the poorest parts of cities are often to be found on steep slopes or low-lying areas close to rivers and swamps. These are areas likely to be affected by landslides or flooding in times of heavy rains, and authorities sometimes prohibit return to such areas after a disaster. Where flooding is becoming more regular and more serious as a consequence of climate change, governments (e.g., in Mozambique) are considering moving whole populations from low-lying lands in river valleys to higher elevations. Evacuations and relocations against the will of affected persons are obviously at odds with the right to liberty of movement and freedom to choose one's place of residence. However, current human rights law does not absolutely prohibit evacuations and relocations. The free consent of persons concerned should be obtained before ordering such measures. Where this is not possible, the right to freedom of movement can be limited if (cumulatively) a law explicitly allows officials to order evacuations, relocations, and prohibition of return; the actual measure serves exclusively the goal of protecting the safety of the persons concerned; and it is necessary and proportional to this end, and only resorted to if there are no other less intrusive measures.[15] Permanent relocations against the will of affected populations are admissible only in very exceptional cases.

Right to Adequate Food, Shelter and Health. These rights aim at ensuring that people who no longer can take care of themselves are provided with adequate humanitarian assistance covering basic needs regarding food, potable water, shelter, and basic health services. According to international human rights bodies, "adequacy" in this context means that these minimum goods and services are *available* to the affected population in sufficient quantity and quality; that they are *accessible*—meaning that they are granted without discrimination to all in need and within safe and easy reach for everyone, including vulnerable and marginalized groups; that they are *acceptable*--culturally appropriate and sensitive to gender and age; and that they are *adaptable* —provided in ways flexible enough to adapt to the changing needs of beneficiaries.[16] In the context of natural disasters, humanitarian aid is usually granted generously, however, its accessibility without discrimination and acceptability is often not ensured.

Right to Education. Particular problems arise where schools are used as emergency shelters for displaced persons. This practice affects the right of education of local children if such use, as is often the case, continues for months or even years. Sometimes, displaced children do not have access to schools in the areas of displacement because they have no personal documentation or other official documents necessary for transfers from one school to another.

Right to Work. This right does not entail an obligation by the state to provide everyone with a job. Rather, it prohibits measures depriving people of access to livelihoods. Furthermore, competent authorities should take measures helping those affected by a

Instructional and Classroom Applications

Grade Level: Middle/High School

Social Studies Standards
⑤ INDIVIDUALS, GROUPS, AND INSTITUTIONS
⑨ GLOBAL CONNECTIONS

To interpret and apply the human rights concepts in this essay to real-life situations, provide students with Internet access to images of natural disasters in the U.S. and other countries. If Internet access is not easily obtainable, then identify selected images and print them for classroom use. Among the websites where such images can be found are those of National Geographic and Save the Children International Alliance.[17] Create student groups with a maximum of 6 participants each. Assign these roles to students (you can pair students for each role if desirable): medical doctor or nurse, local elected official, law enforcement, human rights activist (NGO member), primary school teacher, and local first aid squad member.

Each person should examine the images assigned to him or her and respond to these questions individually: (1) What do you observe as the impact on the community of the natural disaster shown in this photo? (2) From your role's perspective, what would be three key priorities for disaster relief and recov-

ery in responding to the disaster in the photo? (3) Also from your role's perspective, if you knew natural disasters such as this might strike again, what preventive measures would you propose to limit the harm to humans, animals, property, and other aspects of the community?

Once students have written their responses to the questions, distribute a summary of the Operational Guidelines on Human Rights and Natural Disasters (see citation 22 of this article). First, have students share their individual responses to the photos, and discuss how their role-based responses were similar or different. Second, have the small groups compare their responses to the UN guidelines, identify areas where they are in agreement and disagreement, and explore unique concerns noted by the UN and/or students. Third, discuss with the full class the relative prominence of human rights guarantees in their small-group question responses, and the degree to which human rights protections are evident or lacking when compared to the UN Guidelines. As a culminating assessment, student groups should prepare a model set of guidelines for their local government, their school, or a local community organization that will help prepare for natural disasters and embodies human rights concepts. The instructor should review the guideline documents and share them with local leaders to assist in natural disaster preparedness initiatives.

---

disaster, in particular the displaced, to regain their livelihoods. In some countries affected by the Indian Ocean Tsunami, fishing families were reportedly resettled from coastal areas, ending up destitute since no adequate livelihood alternatives were available or made available in resettlement areas. In Central America, although the reconstruction and resettlement itself had been undertaken in a commendable manner after Hurricane Mitch, affected persons continued to be dependent on handouts for many years, whereas before the disaster, they had sustained themselves as day laborers, small-business people, or subsistence farmers. On the other hand, in the United States, city authorities in Houston took active measures to integrate persons displaced from New Orleans into the local labor market by providing them with necessary information and individual counseling.[18]

Right to Personal Documentation. Possession of personal documentation such as birth certificates, identity cards, or (in some countries) social security numbers or drivers licenses is essential to access public services or establish a legal residence. A

lack of legal provisions to quickly and smoothly replace personal documents may create important obstacles when people try to rebuild their lives. For instance, several years after Hurricane Katrina, a backlog of several tens of thousands of birth certificate applications existed in New Orleans due to the destruction of records in the flooding. An example of how such challenges can be dealt with appropriately comes from Sri Lanka, where shortly after the tsunami, regional offices of the Sri Lanka National Human Rights Commission worked with local officials to deploy mobile teams to disaster areas to process requests for replacement documentation.[19]

Property Rights. The destruction of houses and other private possessions is typical for sudden-onset disasters. Persons displaced by such disasters are often confronted with insufficient legal and budgetary frameworks to help them rebuild their properties or access new property. Particular problems are faced by those whose title deeds were destroyed or who had no formal property titles, but possessed land and houses on the basis of customary law or uncontested long-term use. Lack of evidence of property or possession may become an obstacle when trying to access compensation or financial support for the reconstruction of houses.

The Prohibition of Discrimination as Crosscutting Guarantee

The basic prohibition of discrimination is particularly relevant for persons affected by natural disasters. Non-discrimination does not prohibit differential treatment. Rather, it requires that especially vulnerable persons among the displaced (such as children, expectant mothers, mothers with young children, female or minor heads of household, persons with disabilities, persons who are seriously ill or injured, and older persons) are entitled to protection, the assistance required by their condition, and treatment that takes into account their special needs.

In natural disaster situations, discrimination in access to and distribution of humanitarian assistance and reconstruction aid is the major problem. Sometimes, affected persons belonging to a specific ethnic or religious minority may be deliberately disadvantaged by authorities. In most instances, however, discrimination results from neglect by disaster responders in responding to the specific needs of particularly vulnerable categories of persons among affected populations. For instance, specific needs of older persons without family support or persons with disabilities are often simply forgotten. The gender dimension of the consequences of natural disasters also needs to be taken into account. Following the Indian Ocean Tsunami and Cyclone Nargis, it was clear that women were disproportionately affected by the floods. They were more exposed to gender-based violence and abuse in the aftermath.[20] Sometimes distribution schemes utilize gender-based stereotypes, as in the case of a Madagascar village where single mothers with access to land were excluded from the needs assessment lists for seed distribution, based on the assumption that only male farmers would be using the seeds. Both preparedness and response measures should address the specific vulnerabilities women experience in natural disaster situations.

Poverty is another factor increasing the risk of being left out. In New Orleans, evacuation plans were based on the assumption that people would use their private vehicles, thus disadvantaging poor people who didn't own cars. In the aftermath of Hurricane Katrina, reconstruction efforts were guided by considerations of urban planning and economic parameters, rather than criteria based on need and vulnerability. The overwhelming majority of persons who several years later were still displaced from Hurricane Katrina was from socioeconomically disadvantaged areas.

Information from countries hit by the 2004 Tsunami indicated that attempts to use new zoning laws banning construction close to the sea effectively prohibited poor fishing communities from rebuilding their traditional villages, while exceptions were made for the tourist industry, thus opening up beautiful beaches to powerful economic actors.[21]

The Way Forward

To address the problems outlined in this chapter, it is necessary to integrate a human rights perspective into disaster prevention, mitigation, and preparedness measures. Human rights considerations based on the specific vulnerabilities of affected persons should be included in the design of national disaster management policies of both national authorities and humanitarian organizations at the earliest opportunity, and particularly at the contingency planning phase.[22] The integration of a human rights-based approach in the design of national disaster management policies and in humanitarian operations by international agencies and organizations, and the implementation of this approach will enhance the capacities of all concerned actors to address relevant human rights concerns and, therefore, help to prevent and avoid violations. ▨

NOTES

1. Human Rights Committee, *Concluding Observations*, United States of America, UN Doc. CCPR/C/USA/CO/3/Rev.1, 18 December 2006, paragraph 26. The Human Rights Committee is an 18 member expert body monitoring the implementation of the International Covenant on Civil and Political Rights.

2. Committee on the Elimination of Racial Discrimination, *Concluding Observations*, United States of America, UN Doc CERD/C/USA/CO/6, paragraph 31.

3. Walter Kälin, "Natural Disasters and IDPs Rights," in "Tsunami: Learning from the Humanitarian Response," *Forced Migration Review*, Special issue July 2005, 10.

4. See Oli Brown, "The Numbers Game," in "Climate Change and Displacement," *Forced Migration Review*, 31, October 2008, 8 - 9.

5. Walter Kälin and Jörg Künzli, *The Law of International Human Rights Protection* (Oxford: Oxford University Press, 2009), 30.

6. The text of the UN human rights conventions is available at www2.ohchr.org/english/law/index.htm#core.

7. Kälin and Künzli, 96 – 120.

8. UN Doc E/CN.4/1998/53/Add.2, dated February 11, 1998. The Guiding Principles can be accessed at: www.brookings.edu/projects/idp/gp_page.aspx.

9. World Summit Outcome Document, UN General Assembly resolution 60/1 (2005), para. 132; General Assembly resolution 62/153 (2007), para. 10; Human Rights Council resolution 6/32 (2007), para. 5.

10. Examples are available at www.brookings.edu/projects/idp/Laws-and-Policies/idp_policies_index.aspx (last visited on September 18, 2009).

11. Convention on the Rights of Persons with Disabilities of December 13, 2006, available at www2.ohchr.org/english/law/index.htm#core.

12. The examples mentioned below are taken from Report of the Representative of the Secretary-General on the Human Rights of Internally Displaced Persons, Walter Kälin, Addendum, Protection of Internally Displaced Persons in Situations of Natural Disasters, UN Doc A/HRC/10/13/Add.1, March 5, 2009.

13. European Court of Human Rights, *Budayeva and others v. Russia*, Applications nos. 15339/02, 21166/02, 20058/02, 11673/02 and 15343/02, judgment of March 20, 2008.

14. *Ibid.*, paragraph 128.

15. See Art. 12 of the 1966 International Covenant on Civil and Political Rights; available at www2.ohchr.org/english/law/index.htm#core.

16. See Committee on Economic, Social and Cultural Rights, General Comment No. 4, The right to adequate housing (art. 11 (1) of the Covenant, paragraph 8 and General Comment No. 12, The right to adequate food (art. 11), paragraphs 7–13), available at www2.ohchr.org/english/bodies/treaty/comments.htm.

17. See "Natural Disasters" at environment.nationalgeographic.com/environment/natural-disasters and "Emergencies and Disaster Response" at www.savethechildren.org/emergencies. Accessed September 27, 2009.

18. Kälin, *Report of the Representative of the Secretary-General on the Human Rights of Internally Displaced Persons*, paragraph 55.

19. *Ibid.*, paragraph 57.

20. See Tripartite Core Group, "Post-Nargis Joint Assessment" (July 2008), at 26. Available at www.reliefweb.int/rw/RWFiles2008.nsf/FilesByRWDocUnidFilename/ASAZ-7GRH55-full_report.pdf/$File/full_report.pdf; and Oxfam International "Rethinking Disasters" (2008), available at www.oxfam.org.uk/resources/policy/conflict_disasters/downloads/oxfam_india_rethinking_disasters.pdf.

21. Kälin, Rep*ort of the Representative of the Secretary-General on the Human Rights of Internally Displaced Perso*ns, paragraphs 33 and 58.

22. Important tools aimed at sensitizing actors to typical human rights challenges in natural disaster situations are found in the Operational Guidelines on Human Rights and Natural Disasters adopted in June 2006 by the United Nations Inter-Agency Standing Committee, UN Doc A/HRC/4/38/Add.1), available at www.brookings.edu/reports/2008/spring_natural_disasters.aspx.

CHAPTER 12

ENSURING RESPECT FOR THE RIGHTS OF PEOPLE WITH DISABILITIES IN NATURAL DISASTERS

JANET E. LORD AND MICHAEL ASHLEY STEIN

Natural disasters pose considerable dangers for human populations. These dangers are enhanced for people with disabilities, who often have their specific needs neglected during crisis responses. During Hurricane Katrina and its aftermath, people with disabilities were trapped in their homes for days and provided with inadequate medical care in shelters. Many disabled people died as a result. Later, the survivors were often unable to access assistance programs.[1] Both Hurricanes Katrina and Rita demonstrated the failure of U.S. federal-level disaster preparedness for meeting the needs of persons with disabilities. Recent natural disasters abroad, such as the 2004 Asian Tsunami and crises resulting from earthquakes, similarly reveal a failure of humanitarian assistance operations conducted by international agencies to respond appropriately to the needs of disabled beneficiaries.

Thinking about Disability in the Context of Natural Disaster

Emergency situations arising from natural disasters invariably cause human suffering. It is the responsibility of local and national governments and humanitarian assistance organizations to minimize this distress to the greatest extent possible, especially for vulnerable populations. Almost by definition, advance planning is crucial. Yet all too often, governments, humanitarian assistance agencies, and other policy makers fail to adopt a disability perspective in natural disaster humanitarian crisis situations; the disability experience is either neglected completely or overlooked when cast among other vulnerable groups. Remarkably, disabled people themselves and their representative organizations are not consulted in disaster preparedness and planning, resulting in inevitable failures to meet the diverse needs of disabled people in disaster situations.

The Many Adverse Effects of Natural Disasters on People with Disabilities

Natural disasters are a source of disabling conditions of all kinds and can exacerbate or create secondary disabilities for people with disabilities. Disasters are often marked by chaos and displacement, and for people with disabilities, this often includes the break-up of support networks of family and community; displacement or abandonment; and destruction of health, rehabilitation, and transportation infrastructure. Assistive devices and service animals may be lost or left behind. The devastating impact of disasters on the psychosocial well-being of the affected population is also a major risk factor. Proximity to a natural disaster increases the stress level of most people—with and without disabilities—and potentially can have even more deleterious effects on individuals with psychosocial disabilities. Anticipating or experiencing the upheaval caused by natural disasters can engender stress to levels that can manifest in physical or mental reactions, and even mitigate the effect of ameliorative medication.[2]

Unfortunately, responses to natural disasters and humanitarian relief historically have been designed by experts who often lack familiarity with the lived experiences of persons with disabilities. In consequence, these schemes have been designed for the mainstream population, and have not accounted for the needs of persons with disabilities.[3] According to a 2005 report by the National Council on Disability, for example, disaster preparedness and emergency response systems "are designed for people without disabilities, for whom escape or rescue involves walking, running, driving, seeing, hearing, and quickly responding to instructions, alerts, and evacuation announcements."[4] That design flaw has manifested both in the exclusion of persons with disabilities from this programming, as well as the erroneous perception that this kind of exclusion results from an inherent inability among people with disabilities. Thus, advocacy by organizations representing disabled peoples is an essential tool in ensuring that humanitarian assistance programs take into account the specific needs of people with disabilities in their preparation for and response to humanitarian crises. People with disabilities and their representative organizations must participate in all programs designed to reach affected populations in times of crisis. This is for the simple reason that the affected population—here, persons with disabilities—have better information on how to empower and protect themselves than do others.

Barriers to Disability Inclusion in Disaster Preparedness and Response

Hurricanes Katrina and Rita in the U.S. disclosed the numerous barriers that stand in the way of disability inclusion in disaster preparedness and response. The key federal administrative agencies charged with disaster preparedness—the U.S. Department of Homeland Security, the Federal Emergency Management Agency (FEMA), and the Department of Health and Human Services—and the larger effort of federal disaster relief coordination utterly failed in meeting their obligation to provide for the needs of persons with disabilities in those disasters.[5] A multitude of barriers served to undermine the rights of people with disabilities, excluding them from essential and often lifesaving assistance, and otherwise reinforcing their marginalization in the aftermath. Temporary shelters lacked accessible entrances and restrooms; people with disabilities were separated from their families and caregivers, who often provide them support; and evacuees were displaced without assistive technologies. The mainstream relief entities were severely challenged in finding medical necessities including wheelchairs and medication, obtaining Braille and captioned information, and securing personal assistance services. The National Organization on Disability reported that fewer than 30% of shelters had access to American Sign Language interpreters, 80% lacked Telephone Typewriters (TTYs), 60% did not have televisions with open-caption capability, and only 56% had areas where oral announcements were posted.[6] There was no centralized source of disability-related information, and relief workers had not been trained to assist them. Worse, many shelters for people who were displaced and had lost their homes in the disasters turned away disability specialists who offered assistance. For example, disability organizations in Louisiana had difficulty securing permission to enter shelters to identify the needs of evacuees with disabilities and provide them with service referrals.[7]

Ensuring the adequate protection of people with disabilities in natural disasters and other types of emergencies ultimately requires a better integrated and implemented policy approach throughout the federal government. Among the lessons learned from recent disasters is that the needs of the disabled population must be both recognized and integrated into future federal policy planning. Policymakers can only properly target priorities and develop appropriate responses if they first acknowledge the life experience and concerns of persons with disabilities.

While the experience of Hurricanes Katrina and Rita show clearly the inadequacy of U.S. federal-level disaster preparedness for meeting the needs of persons with disabilities, the problem is international in scope. Recent humanitarian emergencies abroad—both natural disasters and crises resulting from armed conflict—have revealed the failure of large-scale assistance operations conducted by international agencies to respond appropriately to the needs of disabled beneficiaries. A United Nations (UN) review of overall humanitarian responses and the Tsunami Evaluation Coalition report found that transparency, communication, and accountability to affected populations were notably lacking in relief efforts.[8] These reviews suggest that humanitarian organizations were largely unprepared and ill equipped to address even the most basic needs of people with disabilities in the provision of shelter, food, water, and health care services.

The experience of tsunami relief efforts in Asia disclosed a number of challenges related to the readiness of large-scale relief operations implemented by humanitarian assistance organizations to respond effectively to the needs of people with disabilities. For example, the Center for International Rehabilitation conducted an assessment of humanitarian assistance in tsunami-affected regions of India, Thailand, and Indonesia.[9] The report found that the majority of temporary shelters were not accessible to people with physical disabilities. The Indonesian government, for example, requested the International Organization for Migration to construct 11,000 semi-permanent homes and shelters for the tsunami-affected population. The design could house up to seven people or be adapted for use as a medical clinic or school. Nevertheless, these structures (including their latrines) were inaccessible to people with physical disabilities. Also in Indonesia, food distribution systems relied heavily on an internal displacement camp system that was inaccessible. Among the many health challenges throughout affected areas, there was a major shortage of assistive devices. Most serious was the lack of mental health or counseling services for disaster-affected populations. Where mental health services were available, they tended to be inaccessible because of a lack of transportation options, or where physically attainable, programs limited their focus to addressing shelter needs.[10]

Using the Human Rights Framework to Protect Life in Times of Natural Disaster

The Asian Tsunami in 2004 and Hurricanes Katrina and Rita in the U.S. served as the trigger for disability advocates to frame the protection of persons with disabilities during natural disasters in human rights terms. These disasters and their devastating impact on the lives of people with disabilities prompted the drafters of the UN Convention on the Rights of Persons with Disabilities (UN Disability Convention) to include a specific provision on protection in times of risk, including natural disasters, in the treaty text.[11] There is thus an emerging recognition that human rights protections must be part and parcel of natural disaster prevention and planning, humanitarian assistance, and rebuilding efforts. International human rights obligations require governments and the international community to ensure that those most affected by disasters are protected and that their human rights are ensured. Indeed, the UN Human Rights Committee has stressed that the protection of the right to life requires that States adopt positive measures designed to protect life. These may include measures to increase life expectancy; decrease infant and child mortality; combat disease; and provide rehabilitation, adequate food, clean water, shelter, and other basic survival needs. In addition to recognizing the rights of persons with disabilities to protection in times of risk situations, the UN Disability Convention recognizes the inherent right to life for people with disabilities and, in addition, requires States Parties to "take all necessary measures" to ensure the enjoyment of that right by disabled people, on an equal basis with others.[12] Article 11 requires positive measures of protection and safety for people with disabilities affected by situations of humanitarian emergencies and risk.[13]

Under the international human rights framework, States have the obligation to respect, protect, and fulfill the right to life of people with disabilities and their right to protection and safety in situations of risk and humanitarian emergency such as natural disasters. In meeting their obligation to *respect* the right of people with disabilities to life, States must refrain from interfering directly or indirectly with disabled peoples' enjoyment of the right to life. States must also refrain from policies that enforce discriminatory practices that may impact their right to life, including in times of humanitarian emergency. The obligation to *protect* includes, among other things, the adoption

of all appropriate legislative, administrative, and other measures to prevent threats to the life of people with disabilities by government officials, as well as third parties. Protective measures could include careful monitoring of all settings where people with disabilities live or receive services, whether publicly or privately operated. Transitioning people with disabilities out of institutions and into community-living situations with appropriate supports would also constitute protective measures. In the context of humanitarian crisis situations, protective measures could include disaster preparedness planning with the participation of people with disabilities and the provision of services that are inclusive of people with disabilities, such as appropriate evacuation procedures, or inclusive refugee assistance programming. The obligation to *fulfill* the right to life and protection in situations of risk requires States to, among other things, adopt positive measures to ensure the enjoyment of the right to life.[14] Such measures might include information campaigns that seek to dispel the myth that people with disabilities have lives "not worth living" or training programs for disaster preparedness and relief workers that include the care of people with disabilities in the general population.[15] Hopeful signs of change are the appointment of a senior disability advisor to oversee disability awareness training within FEMA by the Obama administration in 2009, along with the work of the University of Kansas in the Nobody Left Behind Project,[16] (which provides training and has developed helpful, user-friendly checklists for ensuring disability sensitive disaster response).

Conclusion

In the context of natural disaster, governments and humanitarian assistance organizations are generally working on the assumption that the mere mention of persons with disabilities as one among an array of vulnerable groups in need of protection will lead to results on the ground. However, this generalized recognition has not led to the needs of persons with disabilities being addressed in any consistent and ongoing manner, nor has it provided the specific and detailed type of guidance required to meet the needs of disabled people. Indeed, subsuming disability under the rubric of vulnerable groups at particular risk and in need of protection may also serve to reinforce outmoded conceptions of persons with disabilities as objects to be acted upon, thereby perpetuating medical models of disability. Persons with disabilities and their representative organizations must be recognized as resources essential to the development process and, in particular, as agents in the building of inclusive societies in which rights flourish. Emergency preparedness must include the

Instructional and Classroom Applications

Grade Level: Middle/High School

Social Studies Standards
❶ CULTURE
❺ INDIVIDUALS, GROUPS, AND INSTITUTIONS

Objective
To consider the needs of persons with disabilities in natural disasters and to identify strategies to enhance the protection of the disabled in emergency preparedness

Time
45 minutes

Materials
Chart paper, markers or blackboard and chalk (optional)

1. Ask participants to identify natural disasters that can take place in their community (e.g., blizzards, tornados, hurricanes, earthquakes, floods). List these. Ask the group to create three profiles of people with disabilities in their communities. Encourage diverse profiles, including different ages, disabilities (including psychosocial disability), ethnic minority status, and living arrangements (e.g., living alone, in an institution, with family).

2. Collect the profiles and select a diverse sample for use in role plays.

3. Divide participants into small groups and give each group a profile with these instructions: Your group is going to role-play what might happen during a natural disaster. Choose one of the typical disasters identified in Step 1 to role-play using the profile you have received. What really happens in your community in these crises? For example:
   - Loss of electricity, gas, or water
   - Loss of most forms of communication
   - Loss of assistive devices such as artificial limbs, crutches, hearing aids, and eye glasses
   - Loss of means of transportation
   - Inability to meet basic needs such as food, water, shelter, latrines, and health care services
   - Lack of access to service animals

One person should play the person with a disability and others should develop support (or non-support) roles (e.g., family member, neighbor, police, relief worker, medical personnel). You may choose to role-play a worst-case scenario, a best-case scenario, or both.

4. Ask each group to present its role-play. Afterwards, form a panel of those who took the role of the person with disability, and interview them about their experience.
   - What kinds of response were or would have been helpful in this situation?
   - What kinds of response were or would have been unhelpful?

5. Emphasize that although people with disabilities have a human right to life and States Parties must take specific measures to ensure their protection and safety in emergencies, the needs of people with disabilities are often overlooked in natural disasters and other humanitarian crises.
   - What can be done to ensure protection of this right?
   - Who is responsible to see that this protection is provided?
   - Does your community have a disaster preparedness plan? Does it include such protections?
   - What can you do to help first responders and aid workers to better include disability issues in their work?

6. Assessment: Have each group present a disaster preparedness plan for their school or community, or a checklist of tips for humanitarian workers, that takes into account the needs of persons with disabilities. For examples of checklists, go to the website www.nobodyleftbehind.org.[17]

participation of persons with disabilities themselves.

In the United States, policy makers seem to be growing more attuned to the needs and insights of the disability community. Time will tell, however, if and how the political process allows needed policy changes to be met. Similarly, it remains to be seen if government officials will capitalize on the rebuilding opportunities to create a more inclusive and accessible environment. On the international front, positive steps are also being taken, particularly the adoption of the UN Disability Convention,[18] which makes specific provision for the protection of the rights of disabled persons in natural disasters and other situations of risk, and which requires disability inclusion in foreign assistance programming such as foreign disaster assistance. The UN Disability Convention, as one of the most rapidly ratified human rights treaties ever, is serving as a critical impetus for disability inclusion in disaster assistance. The signing of the UN Disability Convention by the U.S. on July 30, 2009, and the prospect of its eventual ratification by the U.S. Senate, creates additional momentum within the U.S. for working on disability and disaster assistance and many other disability rights issues covered in the treaty.[19] A handful of development agencies have committed themselves to disability-inclusive schemes, including the U.S. Agency for International Development,[20] and global standards to provide direction to less informed actors are being drafted. As with the American situation, it is still unclear how effective these initial efforts will be, and how widely they will be adopted.

Looking forward, the emergence of an international disability rights framework should form the foundation for more thoughtful, disability-specific planning in the humanitarian assistance realm. It is to be hoped that implementation of the UN Disability Convention will serve as the impetus to support the holistic integration of disability into domestic laws and policies, international assistance and cooperation, and most trenchantly, protection of disabled persons in situations involving humanitarian emergencies, including natural disaster. Specific measures to address the needs of persons with disabilities in natural disasters should include school emergency planning and preparedness, both in the construction of schools to withstand natural disasters and in the development of evacuation plans sensitive to the needs of persons with disabilities. Schools have a role to play in developing disaster plans that include all people, and they can assist students and their families in developing individual and family preparedness and mitigation plans. They also provide important meeting spaces for community-based organizations that provide training to community emergency response teams. Recognition of people with disabilities in extreme and

humanitarian circumstances also has the benefit of raising the awareness of public education officials about the disability population. While existing policies and guidelines pertaining to vulnerable populations in humanitarian emergencies purport to apply to a wide range of groups, including persons with disabilities, they fail in their application to guide interventions in the field. Ultimately, the inclusion of persons with disabilities is a critical requirement when planning disaster relief and will avoid future human harm and reduce redevelopment costs. 🖾

NOTES

1. See M. L. Fox, G. W. White, C. Rooney, and C., J. Rowland, "Disaster Preparedness and Response for Persons with Mobility Impairments: Results from the University of Kansas Nobody Left Behind Study," *Journal of Disability Policy Studies*, 17(4), (2007: 196-205 [hereinafter Nobody Left Behind Study]; see also Janet E. Lord, Michael Stein, and Michael Waterstone, "Disability Inclusive Development and Natural Disasters" in Robin Paul Malloy, editor, *Law and Recovery From Disaster: Hurricane Katrina 71* (Syracuse: Ashgate, 2008).

2. National Council on Disability, *Saving Lives: Including People with Disabilities in Emergency Planning*, (Washington, DC: NCD, Sept. 2005) [hereinafter NCD Report], available at www.ncd.gov/newsroom/publications/2005/saving_lives.htm.

3. *Ibid.* See also National Council on Disability Public Consultation, *Homeland Security, Emergency Preparedness, Disaster Relief and Recovery*, (Washington, DC: NCD, May 31, 2007), available at www.ncd.gov/newsroom/publications/2007/ncd_consultant_05-31-07.htm.

4. See NCD Report, "Saving Lives."

5. J. Byzek and T. Gilmer, "Unsafe Refuge: Why Did So Many Wheelchair Users Die on Sept. 11?," *New Mobility*, 13 (2000): 21-22, 24.

6. National Organization on Disability. "New Poll Highlights Need for More Emergency Planning for and by People with Disabilities" (Washington, DC: NOD, 2004), available at www.nod.org/content.cfm?id=1489.

7. *Ibid.*

8. John Cosgrave, *Synthesis Report: Expanded Summary: Joint Evaluation of the International Response to the Indian Ocean Tsunami*, (London: Tsunami Evaluation Commission, 2006), available at www.tsunami-evaluation.org/NR/rdonlyres/2E8A3262-0320-4656-BC81-EE0B46B54CAA/0/SynthRep.pdf.

9. International Disability Rights Monitor, *Disability and Tsunami Relief Efforts in India, Indonesia and Thailand*, (Washington, DC: Center for International Rehabilitation, 2005), available at www.ideanet.org/cir/uploads/File/TsunamiReport.pdf.

10. *Ibid.* at pp. 7, 24, 48-9.

11. Convention on the Rights of Persons with Disabilities, G.A. Res. 61/106, UN Doc. A/RES/61/106 (UN: United Nations General Assembly, Dec. 13, 2006) [hereinafter CRPD], available at www.un.org/esa/socdev/enable/rights/convtexte.htm.

12. *Ibid.* at art. 10.

13. *Ibid.* at art. 11.

14. Janet E. Lord, *et al.*, *Human Rights. YES! Action and Advocacy on the Rights of People with Disabilities*, (Minneapolis: University of Minnesota Human Rights Resource Center, 2007), available at www.humanrightsyes.org.

15. For more on training in relation to disability-inclusive planning, see J.L. Rowland, G.W. White, M.L. Fox, and C. Rooney, "Emergency Response Training Practices to Assist People with Disabilities: Analysis of a Sample

of Current Practices and Recommendations for Future Training Programs," *Journal of Disability Policy Studies*, 7 (2007): 216-222.

16. See White, Rooney, and Rowland, "Nobody Left Behind."

17. See White, Rooney, and Rowland, "Nobody Left Behind."

18. See CRPD.

19. See Michael A. Stein and Janet E. Lord, "Ratify the UN Disability Treaty," *Foreign Policy in Focus* (July 9, 2009), available at www.fpif.org/fpiftxt/6247.

20. See U.S. Agency for International Development, "USAID Disability Policy Paper" (Washington, DC: USAID, 1997) available at pdf.dec.org/pdf_docs/PDABQ631.pdf; see also U.S. Agency for International Development, "USAID Disability Policy – Assistance" (Washington, DC: USAID, 2004), available at www.usaid.gov/about_usaid/disability.

CHAPTER 13

NATURAL DISASTERS AND CHILDREN'S RIGHTS

WILLIAM R. FERNEKES

CHILDREN CONSTITUTE ONE OF THE MOST vulnerable groups affected by natural disasters. This is particularly true when their daily survival is placed in imminent danger as a result of separation from their parents or guardians, or as a consequence of the disruption of essential services, or because of the death or severe injury to their parents or guardians, which obstructs efforts to ensure child safety and well-being. Yet, even though individuals under the age of 18 suffer a disproportionate impact from natural disasters, the universal human rights of children are often not secured when disaster strikes, nor are those rights given sufficient attention by governments during periods of disaster relief and societal reconstruction. This essay examines the impact of natural disasters from the perspective of the universal rights of children, discussing relationships between humanitarian aid systems and the rights of children developed during the 20th century, and the degree of progress that is required to guarantee the rights of children when natural disasters strike.

The Rights of Children: A Universal Imperative

The modern conception of the universal rights of children originated during the 19th century in both Europe and North America, with the first attempt at an international set of uniform standards commencing with five principles enshrined in the *Children's Charter*, authored by Eglantyne Jebb, the leader of Great Britain's Save the Children International Union. Those five principles (strongly influenced by the impact of World War I and contemporary social reform movements concerning juvenile justice, child labor, child poverty, and Progressive education) recognized the disproportionate impact of natural and man-made disasters on children by including this statement: "The child must be the first to receive relief in times of distress."[1] The document focused on protection rights and provision rights, specifically seeking to shield the child from social harms while delivering services permitting the child to develop into a healthy, productive adult. Jebb's direct involvement in providing relief to

refugees and displaced persons during the aftermath of World War I, as well as victims of famine and starvation in the newly-formed Soviet Union and the former Ottoman Empire, led her not only to advocate a set of universal rights for children, but also to initiate the development of an international non-governmental organization—Save the Children, which continues its substantial humanitarian work for children today.

Re-titling the Children's Charter as the "Declaration of Geneva," Jebb succeeded in having it adopted by the newly formed League of Nations in 1924. This document served as a foundation for the much-expanded United Nations "Declaration of the Rights of the Child," proclaimed in 1959. With millions worldwide suffering from the massive cataclysm of World War II, intergovernmental organizations (such as the newly formed United Nations) paid increased attention to the impact of both natural and man-made disasters on children. They created programs of humanitarian aid (such as the creation of UNICEF, the United Nations International Children's Emergency Fund, in 1946), incorporated specific protocols in the Geneva Conventions addressing the impact of war on children, and laid the groundwork for an expanded conception of the universal rights of children through debate and discussion in the United Nations Economic and Social Council, and at the UN Commission on Human Rights. With the unanimous adoption of the Universal Declaration of Human Rights (UDHR) in 1948 by the UN General Assembly, much greater attention was focused on developing an international structure of universal human rights guarantees, with children's rights being integral to that design. As a result, the Declaration of the Rights of the Child was adopted unanimously by the UN General Assembly in 1959. It placed children's rights firmly within the broader conception of universal human rights evident in the 1948 UDHR (which included civil and political, social, economic, and cultural rights) and expanded upon the 1924 Declaration of Geneva by incorporating a preamble and ten principles that broadened the scope of children's rights to include both child protection and a much-expanded approach to child provision. Whereas the 1924 Declaration of Geneva limited provision rights to mitigating child hunger, supplying medical care to children, supporting children who had been orphaned, offering assistance to delinquent children in need of guidance, and providing relief to children "in times of distress," the 1959 Declaration stated much more. Its principles affirmed specifically that the child "shall be entitled from his birth to a name and a nationality" (Principle 3); "shall enjoy the benefits of social security" (Principle 4); "shall whenever possible, grow up in the care and under the responsibility of his parents, and in any case, in an atmosphere of affection and of moral and material security" (Principle 6); shall "be entitled to receive education, which shall be free and compulsory, at least in the elementary stages" (Principle 6); and "shall in all circumstances be among the first to receive protection and relief" (Principle 8). The Declaration also made special provisions for disabled children, stating that "the child who is physically, mentally or socially handicapped shall be given the special treatment, education and care required by his particular condition (Principle 5)."[2] Child protection rights were also enhanced, now incorporating protections against neglect, cruelty and exploitation, human trafficking, harmful and premature participation in the labor force, and discrimination.[3] The document also made clear that the child "shall enjoy special protection, and shall be given opportunities and facilities, by law and by other means, to enable him to develop physically, mentally, morally, spiritually and socially in a healthy and normal manner, and in conditions of freedom and dignity" (Principle 2)—a broad mandate preparing the philosophical groundwork for the 20th century's most comprehensive human rights treaty, the Convention on the Rights of the Child (1989).[4]

Some 20 years after the 1959 Declaration was approved, the United Nations took the next step in the process to guarantee the universal rights of children. Following the call by Poland for a United Nations treaty to mark the International Year of the Child (1979), a working group on the Draft Convention of the Rights of the Child commenced deliberations, and using consensus as its guiding operational principle, gradually developed a comprehensive international treaty to guarantee children's rights. The Convention on the Rights of the Child (CRC) emerged in 1989 and was submitted to the General Assembly for consideration. It was adopted by the General Assembly on November 20, 1989, and was opened for signature by member states of the UN in 1990. Within less than a year, the CRC went into force as an internationally binding UN treaty. In addition to protection and

provision rights, the CRC incorporates an active role for the child as a participant in society, recognizing that "the rights to develop and participate in society" are not restricted to children as a collective group, but also extend to the individual child.[5] As Nigel Cantwell noted, "In that [1959] declaration, children were not recognized as having the right to do or to say anything—they were simply to be provided with certain things or services…and to be protected from certain acts. It is therefore significant that the international community has accepted participation rights as an integral part of this convention."[6] The CRC includes 8 particular articles that relate directly to children's engagement in the broader society and their preparation for active citizenship.[7] These articles are listed below:

- ▶ Article 8: Preservation of identity
- ▶ Article 12: Freedom of expression in matters affecting the child and in judicial and administrative proceedings affecting the child
- ▶ Article 13: Freedom of expression and access to information
- ▶ Article 14: Freedom of thought, conscience, and religion
- ▶ Article 15: Freedom of association and freedom of peaceful assembly
- ▶ Article 16: Freedom from arbitrary or unlawful interference with his or her privacy, family, home, or correspondence
- ▶ Article 17: Freedom of access to information from the mass media
- ▶ Article 29: Education, regarding preparation of the child for responsible life in a free society

With this expanded set of rights guarantees in place, and with all but two states-parties of the United Nations in 2008 having ratified the CRC (the two being the United States of America and Somalia), how effectively does the world community secure these rights for children when natural disasters strike?

Humanitarian Responses to Disaster and Children's Rights
As Gunn has pointed out earlier in this book (see Chapter 2), disasters in the 21st century are not easily subdivided into those purely caused by "natural" forces (tsunamis, earthquakes, volcanic eruptions) versus those originated by human agency. There is increasing evidence that human-environment interaction contributes to both the frequency and severity of contemporary disasters. As documented in a 2008 UN report, since the late 1970s, "the number of natural disasters worldwide is

three to four times higher than 30 years ago" and "175 million children every year are likely to be affected by the kinds of natural disasters brought about by climate change."[8] Cognizant of this trend, examples utilized here are drawn from 1988 to 2008, a time span that approximates the duration of the CRC's existence as a binding international treaty and has witnessed increased attention concerning the plight of children affected by natural disasters. Two topics directly impacting the quality of life in schools are explored—the right to education and the right to adequate health care, with relevant CRC articles noted.

Right to Education (Articles 28-30)

The United Nations has taken the lead in providing guidance to humanitarian relief organizations assisting populations affected by natural disasters, recognizing that the problems are often multifaceted, and thus merit the attention of multiple UN agencies, along with other non-governmental organizations and government departments. UNICEF noted in 2008 that two of the Millennium Development Goals set by the UN in 2000—the achievement of (1) universal primary education and (2) gender equality—are directly affected when disasters disrupt educational services, such as occurred in Myanmar in 2008 following Cyclone Nargis. Working with the Save the Children Alliance, UNICEF coordinated a UN Inter-Agency Standing Committee to restore education in societies affected by emergencies (including natural disasters). UNICEF assisted Myanmar's government in helping to reopen 2,300 schools and 343 early childhood development centers after Cyclone Nargis destroyed 4,000 Myanmar schools and killed over 84,000 people. In the same year, earthquakes in China damaged more than 12,000 schools, killing thousands of children and shaking the confidence of the Chinese population in their government's monitoring of school construction and safety procedures.[9] The importance of restoring education as quickly as possible in safe school environments after an emergency is critical; as stated in the UNICEF 2008 annual report, "School must be a refuge in times of crisis, a place where children can reclaim some sense of normalcy and begin to heal."[10] The guidelines discussed by Kälin (see Chapter 11) reflect a determined effort by the UN to coordinate disaster relief and reconstruction efforts within a human rights framework, and education is clearly one of the most important public services, as the "prompt return to school after natural disasters is important to minimize disruption to the education to which displaced children are entitled and which is also critical for their psychosocial well-being."[11]

In the United States, the devastating impact of Hurricane Katrina (2005), which left over 1,300 people dead and displaced 1 million people from their homes, also produced major disruptions of education for the region's children, leaving over 370,000 students without schools to attend.[12] Despite a massive relief effort over the next year, by the fall of 2006, Save the Children reported that "children still face enormous challenges...Many still live in temporary and often unwelcoming situations. They have lost their communities and schools, disrupting social networks and learning. And studies have found high rates of depression, anxiety and behavioral problems among many children trying to make their way in a post-Katrina world."[13] Recognizing the substantial impact which natural disasters have on children's social-emotional stability, Save the Children's response to Hurricane Katrina encompassed both the provision of material relief to reconstitute school operations and the use of a structured curriculum based on collaborative activities to help them restore a sense of community in their lives while beginning the healing process.[14] This same approach is reflected in the UN Inter-Agency Standing Committee's *Guidelines on Mental Health and Psychosocial Support in Emergency Settings*, which makes clear that children are a high-risk population during emergencies—particularly those who are separated from parents and guardians, subject to trafficking; those who are in conflict with the law, or engaged in dangerous work; and those who are street children or children who suffer from hunger and malnutrition or lack of proper nurturing and stimulation. These children encounter many complex challenges when disasters strike:

- ▸ The intensification of pre-existing social problems (children living in extreme poverty)
- ▸ Dealing with emergency-induced social problems (family separation and loss of social networks)
- ▸ Dealing with emergency-induced psychological problems (grief and depression and/or anxiety disorders)
- ▸ Problems related to humanitarian aid (disruption of traditional community support mechanisms or lack of sufficient information about obtaining aid)[15]

Thus, reopening schools and focusing primarily on their academic mission is clearly insufficient. As these recent UN Guidelines and the work of non-governmental organizations like Save the Children demonstrates, the best interests of children can only be met with a coordinated approach that addresses their social, emotional, and psychological well-being in equal measure.

Instructional and Classroom Applications

Social Studies Standards
⑥ POWER, AUTHORITY, AND GOVERNANCE
⑩ CIVIC IDEALS AND PRACTICES
⑨ GLOBAL CONNECTIONS

Utilizing Hunt and Metcalf's approach to encouraging reflective thought as the core of democratic citizenship education, classroom practitioners can help students examine children's rights in the context of natural disasters as one of the "closed areas" of the social studies curriculum.[16]

Teachers can pose a central question—what is the relationship between the rights of children and the restoration of social stability during natural disasters? Students are then invited to pose subsidiary questions and issues emerging from the central question, and they will then work in small groups to develop their concerns as questions for inquiry. Once definitions of terms are agreed upon by the class, the teacher works with students to develop a hypothesis for investigation. An example is: "When natural disasters strike, the restoration of social order limits the commitment to sustaining the rights of children." Students then apply critical skills of interpretation, analysis, and evaluation to sources that help them examine the hypothesis, pursue answers to their related questions that would help test the validity of the hypothesis, and prepare tentative conclusions based on their investigation. A potential outcome would be a set of policy recommendations for local, county, state, regional, and/or national disaster preparedness agencies and non-governmental organizations to guide public policy development concerning natural disasters and their impact within a human rights context.

Child Health (Articles 23-27)

Another critical UN Millennium Goal addressed the pervasive problem of child survival, setting a target of reducing by two-thirds the under-age-five mortality rate by 2015. By 2005, UNICEF was reporting that Latin America and the Caribbean were the only world regions likely to achieve this goal by 2015, as the world continued to experience more than over 10.5 million deaths annually in the population whose age is under five years old.[17] Since the most critical factor for the under-age-five

population's survival and quality of life is the type of care and protection provided by adults, disruptions to such care from natural disasters can have devastating effects on child health and mortality. Loss of access to potable water, inadequate sanitation, and overcrowding in relief shelters and camps contribute significantly to the spread of diseases which can be lethal to the under-age-five population, as well as to older children. During the aftermath of the huge Indian Ocean Tsunami of December 2004, there was an inconsistent commitment to maintaining high standards of health care in the region, even two years after the event. As Lewis reported, "Two years later, some regions still experience severe shortages in health services and the physicians and nurses to provide them."[18] Compounding the problem is the recognition that restoring the quality of public health requires a commitment to addressing the mental health challenges brought on by natural disasters, particularly the restoration of community support services in affected areas. Similar to the approach taken by the IASC in their *Mental Health and Psychosocial Support Guidelines* document, the same group's *Operational Guidelines on Human Rights and Natural Disasters* incorporates within Guideline B, "Protection of Rights Related to Basic Necessities of Life," a set of six critical subtopics. These subtopics address the provision of adequate goods and services concerning food, water, sanitation, shelter, clothing, and essential health services. And it is significant that Subtopic B. 2.5 states that "Those affected by the natural disaster should be given access to psychosocial assistance and social services, when necessary." Subtopic B. 2. 6 goes on to state that "Special attention should also be given to the prevention of contagious and infectious diseases, including HIV/AIDS, among the affected population, particularly among those displaced by the disaster."[19]

The implementation of these IASC Guidelines has substantial implications in light of recent predictions regarding how climate change processes and natural disasters resulting from climate change can impact children's health. In a 2008 report, Save the Children stated that "Climate change, and the severe natural disasters associated with it, is already affecting the spread and intensity of disease, especially those diseases that affect children."[20] The report notes that the most frequent cause of death among children occurs in the neonatal stage, most often during the first 24 hours of life, and that disruption of health services directly related to supporting life at this stage is acute during natural disasters, particularly when the effects are intensified by increased exposure of the mother and the child to disease and life-threatening conditions.

Aside from the immediate disruption of health services,

disasters such as floods and earthquakes can limit or destroy access to water supplies and sanitation, thus placing children at greater risk of disease and increasing the risk of food insecurity. As Save the Children notes, 3.5 million children per year die from the effects of malnutrition, with one-third of all deaths under five being a result of malnutrition.[21] When exposure to disasters is repetitive (frequent flooding) or of long duration (extended droughts or desertification), the likelihood of chronic malnutrition increases.[22] Consequently, any effort to mitigate or reduce the mortality rate of children under five to meet this UN Millennium Development Goal must address the impending challenges that climate change and natural disasters resulting from it will have on world populations.

Conclusion

Despite the challenges outlined above, efforts are underway by both the United Nations and non-governmental organizations to more effectively develop and coordinate humanitarian relief in response to natural disasters, while paying much more attention to guaranteeing children's rights throughout relief and recovery processes. For the first time, it appears that a systematic and cohesive approach to dealing with the severe impact of natural disasters is possible, particularly if UN states become more effective in developing pro-active disaster response plans, and prepare effectively to address the related impact of natural disasters on human movement (refugees and internally displaced persons), environmental degradation, and the sustainability of essential services to affected populations.[23] If the fundamental rights of children are to be guaranteed, then much work remains to be done in the United States and worldwide, but with momentum developing in the U.S. supporting ratification of the CRC, and with increased attention being directed to emergency preparedness around the world, the potential to secure the rights of children affected by natural disasters is enhanced. If past practice serves as a guide, the defining factor making for change will be the active engagement of citizens across the globe who demand that the future of their children not be compromised by poor planning, inadequate provision of resources, and inattention or indifference to human rights.

NOTES

1. "Declaration of Geneva (1924)," in *Children's Rights: A Reference Handbook*, Beverly Edmonds and William R. Fernekes, eds., (Santa Barbara: ABC-CLIO, 1996), 82-83.

2. United Nations, "Declaration of the Rights of the Child (1959)," in *Children's Rights: A Reference Handbook*, Beverly Edmonds and William R. Fernekes, eds. (Santa Barbara: ABC-CLIO, 1996), 105-108.

3. *Ibid.*, 106-107.

4. *Ibid.*, 106.

5. Beverly Edmonds and William R. Fernekes, "An Introduction to Children's Rights," in *Children's Rights: A Reference Handbook*, Beverly Edmonds and William R. Fernekes, eds. (Santa Barbara: ABC-CLIO, 1996), 10.

6. Nigel Cantwell, "Conventionally Theirs: An Overview of the Origins, Content and Significance of the Convention on the Rights of the Child," *Social Education* 56, no.4 (1992): 209.

7. United Nations, "Convention on the Rights of the Child (1989)," in *Children's Rights: A Reference Handbook*, Beverly Edmonds and William R. Fernekes, eds. (Santa Barbara: ABC-CLIO, 1996), 117-139.

8. International Save the Children Alliance, "Prepare Now for Future Disasters Linked to Global Climate Change, New Report Says," (June 20, 2008) www.savethechildren.org. Accessed July 18, 2009.

9. United Nations Children's Fund, *UNICEF Annual Report 2008* (New York: UNICEF, 2008), 13. Available from www.unicef.org. Accessed July 17, 2009.

10. *Ibid.*, 13.

11. Walter Kälin, "Natural Disasters and IDPs' Rights," *Forced Migration Review* 31 (July 2005): 10.

12. International Save the Children Alliance, "Katrina Response: Protecting the Children of the Storm," *Issue Brief* 2 (September 2006): 1. Available from www.savethechildren.org. Accessed July 18, 2009.

13. *Ibid.*, 1.

14. International Save the Children Alliance, "Helping Children Heal from the Gulf Coast Hurricanes," (September 29, 2005). Available from www.savethechildren.org. Accessed July 18, 2009.

15. United Nations: Inter-Agency Standing Committee, *IASC Guidelines on Mental Health and Psychosocial Support in Emergency Settings* (Geneva: IASC, 2007). Available from www.humanitarianinfo.org/iasc/content/products. Accessed July 18, 2009.

16. Maurice P. Hunt and Lawrence E. Metcalf, *Teaching High School Social Studies, Second Edition*. New York: Harper and Row, 1968.

17. UNICEF, *The State of the World's Children 2005: Childhood Under Threat* (New York: UNICEF, 2005), 9-10.

18. Hope Lewis, "Human Rights and Natural Disaster: The Indian Ocean Tsunami," *Human Rights*, 33, no. 4 (Fall 2006): 14.

19. United Nations: Inter-Agency Standing Committee, *Protecting Persons Affected by Natural Disasters: IASC Operational Guidelines on Human Rights and Natural Disasters* (Geneva: IASC, 2006), 22-23. Available from www.humanitarianinfo.org/iasc/. Accessed July 18, 2009.

20. International Save the Children Alliance, "In the Face of Disaster: Children and Climate Change," (London: International Save the Children Alliance, 2008), 4. Available from www.savethechildren.org. Accessed July 17, 2009.

21. *Ibid.*, 5.

22. *Ibid.*, 5.

23. United Nations High Commissioner for Refugees, "Climate Change, Natural Disasters and Human Displacement: A UNHCR Perspective," (October 23, 2008). Available from www.unhcr.org. Accessed July 18, 2009.

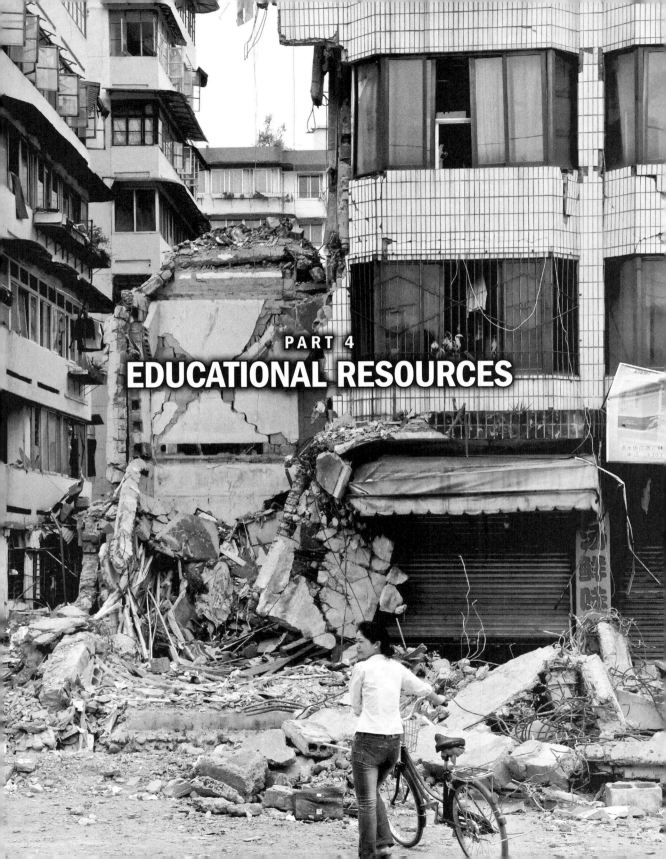

PART 4
EDUCATIONAL RESOURCES

OVERLEAF

A young woman walks with her bicycle amidst the rubble
in the ruins of Han Wang, Sichuan province, China,
after the province was hit by an earthquake in 2004.
Official figures confirm that 34,000 people died. Save
the Children worked closely with the government and
the local Red Cross to help with education and child
protection in the aftermath of the earthquake.

(Colin Crowley/ Save the Children)

CHAPTER 14

NATURAL DISASTERS IN LOCAL COMMUNITIES: GUIDING THE DEVELOPMENT OF GLOBAL CITIZENS IN THE ELEMENTARY GRADES

VALERIE OOKA PANG AND RICHARD OSER

SOCIAL STUDIES EDUCATION HAS MANY PURPOSES.[1] The primary goals of the field include socialization of students, the development of responsible citizens in a democratic society, and the provision of accepted knowledge and skills from a wide range of disciplines. Other main goals include the development of critical inquiry and intellectual freedom, teaching students to question and challenge normative beliefs, and the examination of social issues that are not limited by subject-field boundaries. This contradictory setting (teaching both accepted knowledge and the skills to question and challenge accepted knowledge) is simultaneously the strength and weakness of social studies education. The combination of both offers a rich background of traditional knowledge and cultural orientations of a society, as well as the opportunity to advance that society by addressing its problems, rather than the acceptance of past beliefs and practices.

While social studies students are directed to study and identify aspects of the traditional "common good," individuals and groups do not hold the same values and they may differ on whose interests should be at the core of citizenship and socialization. The "common good" is difficult to define and often not universally accepted.[2] This disparity offers avenues for social studies education to examine social issues from various perspectives and multiple subject fields, and provides opportunities for students to engage in critical thinking.

Natural disasters present numerous social issues. This chapter follows from a special section on natural disasters in the United States published in *Social Education* in 2008.[3] That dialogue is extended to present ways in which elementary grade instruction about local disasters should also include discussion of international human rights. An overview of the global context

for civics education on natural disasters and their connections to human rights is followed by a discussion of a specific disaster (wildfires) and an example of how teachers at one school encouraged students to make connections between the needs of people in their communities and the needs and rights of people around the globe.

Citizenship in a Global Context: The Setting for Education on Disasters and Rights

John Dewey believed that students in schools should be engaged in participatory democracy as young people; they must be able to address complex social problems and act on their decisions.[4] Martha Nussbaum believes that students should grow up seeing themselves as citizens not only of the United States, but also of humanity.[5] National Council for the Social Studies similarly identifies two crucial curricular standards of particular importance to this chapter. Standard 10 focuses on civic ideals and practices reinforcing the importance of an empowered, active citizenry. Standard 9 targets the importance of citizens making global connections and collaborating with others to tackle social issues.

Teachers play a central role in encouraging students in the exploration and examination of local and global democratic ideals, such as the respect for human dignity, freedom, civil rights, and civic responsibility under diverse conditions. Disasters present situations where people find themselves with serious restrictions on basic needs such as shelter, food, and health care, and where human dignity, freedom, and civil rights are sorely tested. In this realm, human rights have a social studies connection to the study of disasters. Though the issue of global human rights continues to be crucial, it is often omitted from classroom instruction.[6] The U.S. does not have a systematic human rights curriculum, and this creates a huge void in student understandings of participatory actions within a global context.[7]

Schools are social spaces; they can prepare students for global citizenship. Social studies education can assist students in cognitive growth in disciplines such as political science, history, and geography, while simultaneously guiding students in ethical development, intellectual inquiry, and civic responsibility. Teachers can mentor students in principled maturity where they cultivate affective skills like empathy and compassion.[8] Empathy relates to the ability of a person to understand the feelings and situation of others; in this way, empathy stresses common humanity and social responsibility.[9] Developmentally, young children have a limited understanding of the feelings of others, but by nine years of age, children can take on the affective role of other people's emotions.[10] Empathy reinforces a bond with others, rather than a feeling of separation; it encourages a prosocial orientation. Social studies teachers can create linkages between what students see as human needs as a result of natural disasters, and the social necessities of international human and children's rights for themselves and others.

Natural Disasters and Human Rights

Natural disasters occur around the world and create severe human hardships. In the aftermath, individuals and families encounter many problems, including losing their homes, difficulty finding food, vulnerability to disease, and trouble securing clean drinking water. Children can face these issues along with their family members. Social studies education is a crucial subject area where students should be encouraged to consider the rights of children, especially in the compelling context of disasters. The UN Convention on the Rights of the Child in 1959 identified a collection of rights that foster the development of human potential; these rights are similar to the Universal Declaration of Human Rights of 1948. However, the Rights of Children are specific to young people under 18 years old. The Convention on the Rights of the Child gave UNICEF (United Nations International Children's Emergency Fund) a legal role to promote and protect child rights. Examples of those rights are: "Children have the right to be protected from being hurt and mistreated, physically or mentally" and "All children have the right to a primary education, which should be free. Wealthy countries should help poorer countries achieve this right."[11] These specifics assist students in understanding the universality of human rights as they discuss the effects of floods, earthquakes, tornadoes, hurricanes, and wildfires on similarly aged children in the United States and elsewhere.

Reluctance on the part of elementary level educators to engage students in issues-centered education is not consistent with social studies goals. All students deserve to better understand social issues, their civic responsibilities, and common humanity with material tailored to their capabilities. One way that schools, parents, and teachers have involved students during difficult times of disasters is to engage them in community service, because volunteerism is valued and encouraged in this country (though not in all countries).[12] As members of a community, the students become part of a united group and work to help others as part of their civic duty and responsibilities. They also gain pride of accomplishment.

An Example of a Local Natural Disaster: Wildfires

Basic knowledge about the natures, sources, and results of disasters can assist students in understanding prevention, preparation, and assistance for individuals caught in their paths. Wildfires were chosen to exemplify this approach because this natural disaster is a persistent issue in the United States.

Wildfires are large fires, often in mountainous areas, and have greatly increased in the western states since 1986.[13] The findings of an extensive research study of 1,166 fires from 1970 to 2003 show that persistent drought and the early melting of snowpacks are significant factors contributing to the increase in wildfires. Previously, snow would linger on mountains into late spring, and this would keep temperatures lower, aiding in fire prevention. However, snowpacks are melting in early spring, feeding brush while temperatures rise. The existence of hundreds of acres of chaparral (dry brush and grass) provides fuel for increasing summer and fall wildfires. Another powerful factor is drying wind, scorching air from deserts and plains; these winds feed fires from a variety of sources such as lightning, unattended embers from campfires, falling electrical lines, mountainous fires, and stray cigarettes. Fires in the United States, particularly in the West, are often burning larger areas and at hotter temperatures.

Wildfires are natural disasters that have impacted not only rural and mountainous regions, but also urban areas. In California, lightning, downed power lines, arson, and careless actions of humans have been the igniting sources of many wildfires in mountainous areas. Hot embers from these fires can travel for several miles, causing large neighborhood fires.

Student Dialogue and Discussion of Human Needs Due to Natural Disasters

Numerous elementary grade children in the United States directly or vicariously have experienced the devastation brought about by wildfires. Students explain their concerns about finding family members, where to live during an evacuation or destruction of the family home, and the loss of personal property to fires. These discussions can begin student dialogue about the needs of people in other countries who also face similar catastrophes—for example, there have been major earthquakes in China, famines in Bangladesh, and tsunamis in Sri Lanka. All of these disasters have led to great human needs and serious questions about human rights.

Children who have experienced local natural disasters can also discuss their fears, insecurities, and problems. Through these conversations, teachers can encourage young students to identify major issues that arise from the destruction brought by natural disasters. Children and their families can identify the survival needs of victims of disaster. The discussion of needs may then turn to rights and the question, "What do children need in order for them to reach their potential?" This can lead students into a dialogue about rights and how societies have addressed the needs and rights of children. These conversations and investigations are expedient avenues from which teachers can make linkages between local and global disasters.[14] The next section describes ways in which educators have empowered students to become active participants in their communities and to consider working with members of other nations.

Case Study: A School's Effort to Promote Global and Local Citizenship

This section of the chapter describes how the California wildfires in San Diego county affected the ongoing efforts of an elementary school, Golden Avenue, in developing strong school-parent partnerships and in mentoring students to become active citizens, locally and globally. These goals were begun in 2005 when a new group of parents took on the leadership of the school's Parent Teacher Association (PTA) in collaboration with teachers and administrators. The PTA wanted to encourage all families to participate in and contribute to the school. The adults knew that this journey would take time and effort. The PTA and school faculty began with various community-building activities, such as a fall learning festival and beautification of the school grounds. The fall learning festival was moderately successful in 2006, with approximately 100 families participating and about 30 parents donating time in the garden project. A 2007 fall festival

was planned; however, it was cancelled when wildfires erupted.

On October 21, 2007, Governor Arnold Schwarzenegger declared a state of emergency in seven counties of California due to wildfires. The counties were Los Angeles, Orange, Riverside, San Bernardino, San Diego, Santa Barbara, and Ventura. During that time, over half a million residents of San Diego County were under mandatory orders to evacuate. The evacuation area was more than sixty miles, from beach communities on the west to rural towns in the east. Evacuees included many children and their families. All schools in San Diego County were closed. As a result of mass mandatory evacuations and intolerable air quality, almost half a million students stayed home for more than a week. Local media coverage was relentless, leaving lasting images, fear, and insecurities in the minds of many San Diego County residents. While adults attempted to understand the gravity of the situation, manage their own fears, and balance work and childcare responsibilities, many children were left alone to grapple with their emotions and lasting memories of the devastation.

At Golden Avenue Elementary in San Diego County, where almost 50% of the students reported that they "seldom or never feel safe outside of school," educators faced dual challenges. First, the school personnel had to address the immediate impact of the natural disaster. Second, they had to rebuild the inclusive, positive school climate that had been an objective for the past two years. Golden Avenue Elementary had demographics like many urban schools—78% of the students qualified for free or reduced lunch status, and high mobility resulted in the demographics changing significantly in the past 16 years. Many of the students were immigrants with strong ties to relatives and friends in Mexico; their experiences demonstrated the fluid nature of globalism.

After the San Diego wildfires, the school's faculty took immediate action to help students and families address their fears and insecurities. Teachers encouraged students to express their worries through open dialogue in the classroom, personal conversations, and written reflections. Students shared their feelings of isolation and powerlessness. Many English learners did not know how close or far the wildfires were to them, increasing their fears. Some students worried about their cousins and grandparents in Mexico, who were also threatened by wildfires. Throughout these discussions, teachers and staff reinforced a strong sense of community and acceptance of everyone. Since many students were close to families in Mexico, teachers also led discussions about the needs of children from other disaster regions in the world. For those students who were most traumatized by the wildfires,

Instructional and Classroom Applications

Social Studies Standards

⑨ GLOBAL CONNECTIONS

Challenge learners to analyze the causes, consequences, and possible solutions to persistent, contemporary, and emerging global issues.

⑩ CIVIC IDEALS AND PRACTICES

Help learners to analyze and evaluate the influence of various forms of citizen action on public policy.

As part of the unit, teachers and students can identify core questions that guide the instructional activities.

Possible Focal Questions for Lessons or Units

▸ Who should help our local neighbors during a natural disaster? Why?

▸ What should be our priorities during natural disasters? Why?

▸ Who should help our global neighbors during a natural disaster? Why?

▸ What are children's rights and can they be linked to natural disasters? If not, why not? If so, how?

▸ Which children's rights are most important during a natural disaster? Why?

▸ What responsibility does an individual person have towards others faced with a natural disaster?

Possible Activities

After focal questions have been identified, students can begin researching issues to be addressed. Students can write essays identifying their feelings when they encountered a natural disaster, explaining how they felt, what they did, and what could be done in the future to support victims of natural disasters. They could also write about how other students may feel during a natural disaster, and how their experiences were the same or different from their own.

Students can compare their needs with children from another country who have also suffered from a natural disaster. In this way, they can use a Venn diagram to identify and analyze similarities and differences. The children can also discuss what responsibilities citizens have to each other. In this process, students can research Children's Rights, and they can discuss which problem is most important to address. Then students can suggest ways that they could take action to assist and collaborate with children from other countries.

---

support staff (including the school social worker, psychologist, and principal) met with individual students and families, and provided counseling for students.

Just as Norman recommended in Chapter 4, when students returned to school, the teachers and staff worked to return the school to its normal routine. One of the first events was a re-scheduled assembly. Two weeks later, the fall festival took place. This event had a Halloween theme and included learning booths. PTA board members called parents to attend—as a result, over 200 families (about 75% of the school) attended the festival. In addition, there was a 50% increase in the number of Spanish-speaking parents participating, compared to the previous year.

Several months after the disaster, the PTA and school personnel continued to build on their community-service theme. First, the school sponsored a Relay for Life project in conjunction with the American Cancer Society. In 2006, only 29 parents had participated, but after the fires, 87 adults volunteered to raise funds and raced in the event. The school was becoming the center for the neighborhood.

The community momentum evolved into the theme of Mahatma Gandhi's quote, "Be the change you wish to see in the world." Teachers asked their students how they might help each other in being that change. The students answered that they wanted to work together to make the school a more beautiful place—they wanted areas to sit in the main courtyard of the school. Therefore, the school community began with several small service projects, including the construction of a Peace Garden that transformed the entrance of the school into a safe haven complete with murals, garden beds, arbors, benches, and a gazebo. This project was a collaborative effort among the school's Student Council, local businesses, and families. The Peace Garden was a large undertaking, and parents took much of the responsibility in getting materials donated from local businesses. The project had an empowering effect on students, who showed off their gardens to school visitors.

Building on Gandhi's philosophy, one of the most popular activities at the school was the writing of essays that answered the question, "How Can I Be the Change I Want To See in the

World?" Student essays were written throughout the grades, and many papers were hung in the office for everyone to read. Students, parents, and teachers were proud of the ideas the project elicited because the essays demonstrated the strong bonds children felt with others and how the youngsters had become engaged in helping their community.

Momentum from the Peace Garden project carried over to a school-wide effort to put together "Peaceable Packages" for local homeless people. Students became aware of basic needs that homeless individuals lacked in their neighborhood after the fire. This resulted in the Student Council of fourth and fifth graders leading the "Peaceable Packages" effort; students and families from all grade levels donated personal necessities such as new socks, sweatshirts, blankets, toothpaste, toothbrushes, and soap. Students, family members, and volunteers assembled 100 "Peaceable Packages" and then delivered them to a local nonprofit agency. Each class donated an average of 7 packages, and the next year, the Student Council set a goal of 10 packages per classroom.

In March 2009, a year and a half after the San Diego wildfires, the school-wide initiative took a significant stride forward. The PTA and school faculty wanted to create a yearly community-service project that focused on civic engagement. Led once again by the Student Council, "A Day of Service in Honor of Cesar Chavez" was implemented. The "Day of Service" consisted of students, family members, and volunteers participating in a variety of projects around the school and community, including the creation of a mural etched with "Be the change you wish to see in the world." As the collection of students, family members, and volunteers worked in the hot sun, one new parent to the school arrived and immediately asked the principal, "¿Cuando va a empezar la fiesta?" (When is the party going to start?) This parent shared that at her children's previous school, César Chávez Day was celebrated with a fiesta full of food, music, and games. The responding explanation was that another way to honor César Chávez was to conduct a day of service; a family member recruited this parent to join them in painting the school. After hours of working in the heat with her children and other families, the parent returned to express her desire to help the school in any way possible in the future.

The natural disaster created a context where family volunteerism and teaching students civic responsibility to local and global communities was strengthened. As a result, student decision-making has expanded to address a global concern. The elementary school has a partnership with the University of California, San Diego (UCSD), School of Medicine. The

Student Council found that their UCSD partners held an annual medical clinic in the Fiji Islands, where people in many of the islands also need educational supplies. So the students collect books and the school donates older textbooks that are taken to the Fiji Islands by UCSD medical students. The children are growing vegetables in the school's garden, which they will sell at the school, along with homemade salsa. The funds raised will purchase supplies such as pencils, paper, and science materials (litmus paper, magnifying glasses, magnets) for schools in the islands.

The school has chosen empowered citizenship and community-service as major goals for their students, and the elementary grade students at Golden Avenue understand education as a right around the world for young people like themselves. The development of strong local and global citizens does not occur in one or two years; teachers and parents must work continually and consistently with students to engage them in community-service projects. The school reaction to the wildfires reinforced what had already been put in place; the natural disaster acted to put more focus on the importance of community building and active citizenship. The faculty at this school would like to continue with their citizenship focus; however, one of the continuing pressures that the teachers and administrators face is the nation's narrow focus on math and reading scores. If, in the future, the school does not reach the academic performance benchmarks set by the state, the faculty will be forced to eliminate most of the citizenship building and community-service activities.

Conclusion: Local and Global Citizens

The development of empowered local and global citizens is an ongoing journey. Natural disasters create difficult conditions for children and their families; however, schools can mentor students to address social issues. In this process, students should be guided to consider the linkages between human needs and human rights on local and global levels. Social studies education can integrate the issues of human dignity, human needs, and human rights in lessons that teach elementary students to think about their civic responsibilities to others in their own cities and around the world. 🔊

Notes

1. Jack L. Nelson, "Communities, Local to National, as Influences on Social Studies Education" in *Handbook of Research on Social Studies Teaching and Learning*, ed. James Shaver (New York: Macmillan, 1991): 332-341.

2. *Ibid.*, p. 332.

3. Valerie Ooka Pang, Marcelina Madueño, Miriam Atlas, Tamiko Stratton, Jennifer Oliger, and Cindy Page, "Addressing Student Trauma in the Wake

of the California Wildfires," *Social Education* 72, no. 1 (January 2008): 18-23; Dana Riggs, Marcelina Madueño, and Miriam Atlas, "How Schools Can Help: California Teachers Recall the Wildfires," *Social Education* 72, no. 1 (January 2008): 24-26; Ilene R. Berson and Michael J. Berson, "Weathering Natural Disasters with a Net of Safety," *Social Education* 72, no. 1 (January 2008): 27-30.

4. John Dewey, *Democracy and Education* (New York: The Free Press, 1916).

5. Martha C. Nussbaum, *Cultivating Humanity: A Classical Defense of Reform in Liberal Education* (Cambridge, Mass.: Cambridge University Press, 1997).

6. William Gaudelli and William Fernekes, "Teaching about Global Human Rights for Global Citizenship: Action Research in the Social Studies Curriculum," *Social Studies* 95, no. 1 (January 2004): 16-26.

7. *Ibid.*

8. Kathryn P. Scott, "Achieving Social Studies Affective Aims: Values, Empathy, and Moral Development" in *Handbook of Research on Social Studies Teaching and Learning*, ed. James Shaver (New York: Macmillan, 1991), 357-369; Valerie Ooka Pang, *Multicultural Education: A Caring-centered, Reflective Approach* (California: Montezuma Publishing, 2010).

9. Diane J. Goodman, "Motivating People from Privileged Groups to Support Social Justice," *Teachers College Record* 102, no. 6 (December 2000): 1061-1085.

10. Martin L. Hoffman, "Personality and Social Development," *Annual Review of Psychology* 28 (January 1977): 295-321.

11. UNICEF, "Fact Sheet: A Summary of the Rights under the Convention on the Rights of the Child," (Retrieved on May 10, 2009), www.unicef.org/crc/files/Rights_overview.pdf.

12. Carole Norman, Red Cross of San Diego County Consultant. Personal correspondence, June 13, 2009.

13. A. L. Westerling, H.G. Hidalgo, D.R. Cayan, and T.W. Swetnam, "Warming and Earlier Spring Increase Western U.S. Wildfire Activity," *Science* 313 (2006): 940-943.

14. William R. Fernekes, "The Convention on the Rights of the Child: A Critical Imperative," *Social Education* 56 (1992): 203-204.

CHAPTER 15

TEACHING ABOUT NATURAL DISASTERS AND HUMAN RIGHTS: HOW TO PROMOTE STUDENTS' KNOWLEDGE AND SKILLS

MARK A. PREVITE

CORE DEMOCRATIC VALUES require effective citizens to use critical thinking in the study of issues. The examination of natural disasters and investigation of questions relating to the human rights of disaster victims offer a rich opportunity for students to engage in critical inquiry and the skills of effective citizenship.

In classes, students can become confused and indifferent when they perceive no relationship between their lives and the content under study. They sometimes treat their lessons as simply a long trivia game. However, student interest is necessary for learning, and it can be stimulated and developed when social issues are the focus of teaching and learning. The study of issues can provide strong connections between subject knowledge, personal experience, and social responsibility.

Engle reminds us that memorization and regurgitation, the bane of social studies teaching, should be replaced with a proactive social studies that challenges students to confront problems and issues by gathering and evaluating data, drawing conclusions, and analyzing alternative solutions and their potential consequences.[1] The study of disasters is well suited to these objectives. It can also advance another goal of social studies, which is to achieve disciplinary integration. The works of the Rugg brothers from the 1920s through the 1940s, Alan Griffin and his students at Ohio State in the 1940s and 1950s, the Indiana Experiments of the 1960s, and the Harvard consortium during the 1960s and early 1970s were prime models of interdisciplinary social studies, with social issues as a focus. In contrast to these objectives, it is common for social studies classes to provide students only with the experience of remembering facts in one subject field and to offer little familiarity with critical thinking or cross-discipline study of issues.[2]

Examining the nexus between disasters and human rights issues offers a learning experience that can help integrate the knowledge and methods of many disciplines.

It is possible to teach about disasters at all grade levels. Elementary social studies classrooms can operate on an issues-centered approach, where teachers and students alike pose historical and current questions, including questions about the connections between human rights and natural disasters.[3] Elementary students are sometimes so overwhelmed with the auditory and visual sensations of the media coverage of natural disasters that they become weary and distracted; an issues-oriented approach to disaster study can provide a link to the student's personal life, to local and global community life, and to our civic responsibilities. Teaching about disasters also offers necessary citizenship practice in critical thinking. Engle and Ochoa stipulate that independent thinking and social criticism, otherwise known as "counter-socialization," could commence in the elementary years when students possess sufficient maturity and intelligence.[4] Lintner advocates questions that emphasize individual civic responsibility from an interdisciplinary perspective:

> How do you think children who lost their homes feel? How did these natural disasters change where people work, live, and go to school? What infrastructural changes may result from these disasters? Whom should citizens listen to? Why is it important to listen to authorities after a natural disaster? What would happen if we didn't have rules or didn't follow them? What is my civic responsibility to other human beings? Would you want someone to help you? What kind of help would you need?[5]

In an issues-centered environment in middle and high schools, questions "coming from human issues are more significant than the possible answers produced by any single subject."[6] Teaching from an issues-centered philosophy should cause teachers to rethink their traditional classroom environment. In addition to the standardized textbook, multiple sources of information that reflect conflicting evidence and divergent points of view help students address biases, diverse vantage points, and conflicting interpretations. Students should constantly question their sources of evidence, including their teachers, about the relevance of the curriculum to their own lives. The practice of using a textbook as the single, authoritative source seldom leads to critical thinking or to student motivation to engage in study of the issue.[7] Questioning the text, the teacher, and other evidence sources can assist in critical thinking and student ownership of the issue.

Ochoa-Becker proposes five types of questions (definitional, evidential, speculative, policy, and value) for student thinking.[8] For example, using the integration of human rights and disasters:

- ▶ What is the meaning of human rights? (Definitional)
- ▶ What human rights come into play when citizens are impacted by a natural disaster? (Evidential)
- ▶ What should government do when human rights are infringed upon after a natural disaster? (Policy)
- ▶ Are there justifiable reasons for citizens to avoid involvement in any human rights issue related to a natural disaster? (Value)
- ▶ What position would you take if your town or city was designated as a resettlement area for victims of a natural disaster? (Speculative)

Natural Disasters, Human Rights, and Issues-Centered Instruction

Proponents of an issues-centered version of teaching about natural disasters and human rights envision social studies from a viewpoint that would engage them in the ongoing reconsideration of social problems as a basis for civic engagement.[9]

Natural disaster lesson plans located in the ERIC database indicate that the most frequent concepts to be taught to students are a) survival strategies, b) disaster prevention and solutions, and c) coping with tragedy.[10] One particular social studies plan instructs the teacher to provide newspapers for the students to locate examples of social justice, provide a definition of social justice from the research findings, and then reach a consensus from the numerous definitions. The discussion then shifts to the issues, which include preventing the spread of disease, grief counseling, rebuilding economically depressed areas, and the threat of water damage—and their collective impact on the human condition.[11] Taking responsibility for the welfare of others

is a strong indicator of an effective citizen. Many times in the course of a natural disaster, individuals and groups stepped up to provide a helping hand for victims. A group of 7th graders from Washington took this value to heart when their own local geography provided opportunities to teach the members of their community. Using primary and secondary sources, the students designed an interdisciplinary disaster-preparedness media campaign to inform senior citizens about what to do during a volcano eruption and subsequent landslides.[12]

Tolerance.org provides lesson plans for elementary, middle, and high school students to sharpen their analytical skills as they read about the experiences of their peers during the Dust Bowl of the 1930s and Hurricane Katrina in the 2000s.[13] Elementary students hypothesize about the living conditions in a camp of the 1930s or attending a school in the New Orleans area where they contend with issues of evacuation and adjustment to a dissimilar environment and new people. Middle school students compare and contrast photos from both time periods, and then develop and write about pertinent questions on the subject of survival. High school students analyze the vantage points of U.S. farmers and Gulf Coast survivors through the use of primary-source documents and artwork emphasizing issues of poverty, migrant workers, family, and an unknown future.

The NCSS Notable Social Studies Trade Books for Young People offer alternatives to the dry tomes that are often used in elementary and secondary classrooms. These works help K-12 students consider significant issues and provide plenty of questions and in-depth information that the pages of a textbook couldn't provide. During the recent years of the program, three works stand out that can provide students with a powerful message about the centrality of human rights in the work of citizens.[14] In one of these, Palser invites her readers to evaluate the authenticity and reliability of numerous primary source accounts in the days and months after Hurricane Katrina.[15]

One avenue for integrating disaster education with human rights issues is through teacher education programs in which preservice teachers choose a human rights organization whose rationale is to protect the rights of the displaced and disaffected after a natural disaster occurs. Selection of an issue and organization dedicated to that issue, researching the organization, and authoring an advocacy letter to the media about that organization would impress future teachers about the level of action that must be taken to create change.[16] One useful website to support these endeavors is the iEarn Collaboration Centre, through which students from around the world can meet online to discuss and deliberate about the effects of natural disasters in their local communities, which sharpens their present and future decision-making and leadership skills.[17]

Conclusion

Educators are persistently reminded to place greater emphasis on critical thinking, but a focus on subject-field information and basic skills unfortunately often win the day over inquiry, analysis, synthesis, and evaluation in today's classrooms. Developing effective citizens is an enduring process in the eyes of issues-centered educators. The active and intellectual examination of issues offers connections among subject fields, among topics, and with student experiences and emotions; it is "doing democracy" as advocated by Dewey and his followers.

The vision of an issues-centered classroom that focuses on reflective thinking, decision making, debate, and deliberation continues to persist, possessing immense potential as an instructional and curricular model nurturing students to develop into effective citizens.

Social studies education does not end with the final bell of each school day. Teachers must consider questions that include the following: How do our students act when they move beyond the schoolyard? Do they put our teaching into practice? Do our students engage in taking action to assist others in times of need? Does student behavior reflect democratic values and principles? Education about natural disasters and their human rights implications can facilitate all these goals. If public decision-making is at the heart of a democratic society, then public deliberation should be the foundation of the social studies classroom, and issues-centered education is the most effective pathway for learning about and practicing democracy. 🔅

NOTES

1. Shirley H. Engle, "Decision Making: The Heart of Social Studies Instruction," *Social Education*, 24 (3) (November 1960): 301-304, 306.

2. S. H. Engle, "The Commission Report and Citizenship Education," *Social Education*, 54 (7) (November/December 1990): 431-434.

3. See K. E. Koeppen, "It Threw Me for a Loop!: Preservice Teachers' Reactions to Issues-centered Social Studies in the Primary Grades," *Journal of Early Childhood Teacher Education* 22 (3) (2001) 191-199; A. Ochoa-Becker, "A Search for Decision Making in Three Elementary Classrooms," *Theory and Research in Social Education* 29 (2) (Spring 2001): 261-289; and D. Skeel, "An Issues-Centered Elementary Curriculum," in R. W. Evans and D. W. Saxe, eds., *Handbook on Teaching Social Issues* (Washington, DC: National Council for the Social Studies, 1996), 230-236.

4. S. H. Engle and A. S. Ochoa, *Education for Democratic Citizenship: Decision Making in the Social Studies* (New York: Teachers College Press, 1988).

5. T. Lintner, "Hurricanes and Tsunamis: Teaching about Natural Disasters and Civic Responsibility in Elementary Classrooms," *The Social Studies* 97 (3) (May/June 2006): 101-102.

6. J. L. Nelson, "The Historical Imperative for Issues-Centered Education," In R. W. Evans, & D. W. Saxe, eds., *Handbook on Teaching Social Issues* (Washington, DC: National Council for the Social Studies, 1996), 19.

7. John Dewey, *Democracy and Education* (New York: The MacMillan Company, 1916).

8. A. Ochoa-Becker, *Democratic Education for Social Studies: An Issues-centered Decision-Making Curriculum* (Greenwich, CT: Information Age Publishing, 2007).

9. S. H. Engle, "Alan Griffin, 1907-1964," *Journal of Thought* 17 (3) (Fall 1982): 49.

10. See S. Fuhrmann,, L. Stone, M. C. Casey, M. D. Curtis, A. L. Doyle, B. D., Earle, *et al.*, "Teaching Disaster Preparedness in Geographic Education," *Journal of Geography*, 107 (3) (May 2008): 112-120; E. R. Hinde, "Revisiting Curriculum Integration: A Fresh Look at an Old Idea," *The Social Studies*, 96 (3), (May/June 2005): 105; and A. A. Zevenbergen, E. A. Singler, L. J. Duerre, and E. Howse, "The Impact of a Natural Disaster on Classroom Curricula," *Journal of Educational Thought* 34 (3), (December 2000): 285-304.

11. "Educational Moments," *Curriculum Review* 43 (December 2003): 8.

12. J. Kooser, "Volcano Safety for Senior Citizens," in R. C. Wade, ed., *Community Action Rooted in History: The CiviConnections Model of Service-Learning* (Silver Spring, MD: National Council for the Social Studies, 2007), 57-58.

13. C. O'Brien, (September 2006). "Lesson Plans: From Dust Bowl to Katrina." Retrieved June 30, 2009, from www.tolerance.org/teach/current/event.jsp?ar=699.

14. See G. L. Karwoski, *Tsunami: The True Story of an April Fool's Day Disaster.* (Plain City, OH: Darby Creek Publishing, 2006); B. Palser, *Hurricane Katrina: Aftermath of a Disaster* (Minneapolis, MN: Compass Point, 2006); and S. Tanaka, *A Day that Changed America: Earthquake!* (New York: Hyperion Books, 2004).

15. B. Palser, *Hurricane Katrina*, 11-12, 26, 29, 31, 33.

16. R. Wade, "Teaching Preservice Social Studies Teachers to Be Advocates for Social Change," *The Social Studies* 94 (3) (May/June 2003): 129-133.

17. See https://media.iearn.org

CHAPTER 16

RESOURCES FOR SOCIAL STUDIES EDUCATORS ON NATURAL DISASTERS AND HUMAN RIGHTS

WILLIAM R. FERNEKES

Books and Journal Articles

Aguilar, Pilar and Gonzalo Retamal. "Protective Environments and Quality Education in Humanitarian Contexts." *International Journal of Educational Development*, 29, 2009: 3-16.

Carmalt, Jean Connolly. "Rights and Place: Using Geography in Human Rights Work." *Human Rights Quarterly*, Vol. 29, Issue 1, February 2007: 68-85.

Davies, Edward. *Science in the Looking Glass*. New York: Oxford University Press, 2004.

Edmonds, B. and W. R. Fernekes. *Children's Rights: A Reference Handbook*. Santa Barbara: ABC-CLIO, 1996.

Edmonds, B. and W. R. Fernekes, guest editors. Special section on "The Rights of the Child." *Social Education*, Vol. 56, No. 4, April/May 1992: 203-235.

Enarson, Elaine and Betty Hearn Morrow, editors. *The Gendered Terrain of Disaster: Through Women's Eyes*. Westport, CT: Praeger, 1998.

Ernst, G. G. J. and J. Marti, editors. *Environmental Effects of Volcanic Activity*. Cambridge, United Kingdom: Cambridge University Press, 2005.

Gladwell, Malcom. *Tipping Point*. Boston: Back Bay Books, 2002.

Grescoe, Taras. *Bottomfeeder: How to Eat Ethically in a World of Vanishing Seafood*. New York: Bloomsbury USA, 2008.

Haggett, Peter. *Geography: A Global Synthesis*. Harrow, England: Pearson Hall, 2001.

Hess. D. E. *Controversy in the Classroom: The Democratic Power of Discussion*. New York: Routledge, 2009.

Hubbard, Dean. "What Kind of Globalization? Organizing for Workers' Human Rights." *Working USA*, Vol. 9, No. 3, 2006: 315-335.

Kristof, Nicholas D. and Sheryl WuDunn. *Half the Sky: Turning Oppression into Opportunity for Women Worldwide*. New York: Knopf, 2009.

Mattick, Paul. *Social Knowledge*. Armonk, NY: M. E. Sharpe, 1986.

McNeil, William. *Plagues and Peoples*. Garden City, NY: Anchor Books, 1976.

Nelson, Jack, L. and Vera Green, editors. *International Human Rights*. New York: Coleman Press/Human Rights Publishing Group, 1980.

Nieto, Jesus and Valerie Ooka Pang. "Abuses of Children's Rights: Implications and Teaching Strategies for Educators." *Radical Pedagogy*, 2005. radicalpedagogy.icaap.org/content/issue7_2/nieto.html

Redlener, Irwin. *Americans At Risk*. New York: Knopf, 2006.

Sachs, Carolyn E. "Going Public: Networking Globally and Locally." *Rural Sociology*, 72, No. 1, 2007: 2-24.

Sarewitz, Daniel, Roger A. Pielke, Jr., and Radford Byerly, Jr., editors. *Prediction: Science, Decision Making and the Future of Nature.* Washington, DC: Island Press, 2000.

Siegel, Marc. *False Alarm: The Truth about the Epidemic of Fear.* New York: John Wiley, 2006.

Sieh, Kerry. "Aceh-Andaman Earthquake: What Happened and What's Next?" *Nature,* Vol. 434, No. 7033. 2005. www.nature.com/nature/journal/v434/n7033/full/434573a.html

Smith, Dan and Janani Vivekananda. *A Climate of Conflict: The Links between Climate Change, Peace and War.* London: International Alert, 2007.

Sphere Project. *Humanitarian Charter and Minimum Standards in Disaster Response.* Oxford, United Kingdom: Oxfam, 2000.

Thomas, Gregory. *Freedom from Fear.* New York: Random House, 2005.

Tibbitts, F. "On Human Dignity: The Need for Human Rights Education." *Social Education* 60, no. 7 (November-December 1996) 428-431.

UNICEF. *The State of the World's Children 2005: Childhood under Threat.* New York: UNICEF, 2005.

Curriculum Guides and Teaching Units

American Red Cross. Disaster Education: Masters of Disaster Preparedness Curriculum. (Grades K-8). www.redcross.org/disaster/masters

Fernekes, William R. "Why Study Children's Rights?" Global Citizen 2000. gc2000.rutgers.edu/GC2000/MODULES/CHILD_RIGHTS/default.htm

Foundation for Teaching Economics. Curriculum Unit on the Economics of Natural Disasters (Middle and Secondary Grades). www.fte.org/disasters

Hunterdon Central Regional HS, Flemington NJ. "Natural Disasters in U. S. History Research Investigation." Contact lsproul@hcrhs.k12.nj.us to obtain the lesson plan and related materials.

National Oceanographic and Atmospheric Administration. Educational Resources on Natural Disasters. www.education.noaa.gov/weather-html

Teach Engineering, Resources for K-12. Curriculum unit on natural disasters (Grades 3-5). teachengineering.org

Teaching the Levees: Resources to Support Democratic Dialogue and Civic Engagement. Curriculum Guide (Middle and Secondary Grades). www.teachingthelevees.org

UN Cyberschoolbus. Stop Disasters! Online disaster simulation game from the UN/International Strategy for Disaster Reduction. www.stopdisastersgame.org/enhome.html

UN Works. What's Going On? Child Refugees in Tanzania. Lesson Plan: Refugees. www.un.org/works/Lesson_Plans/WGO/WGO_LP_RT.pdf

University of Illinois Extension Division. Children, Stress and Natural Disasters. Curriculum and instruction resources dealing with the impact of natural disasters. (Elementary - Secondary Grades). web.extension.uiuc.edu/disaster/teacher/teacher.html

Electronic Resources:

CD-ROMS, Discussion Boards, Electronic Journals, Online Databases, and Websites
Abramovitz, Janet. "Unnatural Disasters—Worldwatch Paper 158." *World Watch Institute, Worldwatch Paper 158* (October 2001). www.worldwatch.org/system/files/EWP158.pdf

Arctic Monitoring and Assessment Program. Consortium of eight northern hemisphere nations reporting on developments in Arctic melting and its impact on global climate change. www.amap.no

Brymer, Melissa, Anne Jacobs, Christopher Layne, Robert Pynoos, Josef Ruzek, Alan Steinberg, Eric Vernberg, and Patricia Watson. "Psychological First Aid." 2006. www.ptsd.va.gov/professional/manuals/manual-pdf/pfa/PFA_2ndEditionwithappendices.pdf

Johnson, C. G. (2006). *National Issues Forum.* Retrieved May 2, 2009, from "Hurricane Katrina Relief: What Do We Do Now?" www.nifi.org/discussion_guides/detail.aspx?catID=15&itemID=5787

The Journal of Humanitarian Assistance: Field Experience and Current Research on Humanitarian Action and Policy. http://jha.ac

Muhammad Yunus: Nobel Peace Prize Acceptance Speech. nobelpeaceprize.org/en_GB/laureates/laureates-2006

Muhammad Yunus: website. www.muhammadyunus.org

Relief Web. Contains section on website dealing with the impact of natural disasters on children's rights. www.reliefweb.org

The State of The World's Refugees 2000: Fifty Years of Humanitarian Action. www.unhcr.org/4a4c754a9.html

TakingITGlobal. Online community of youth interested in global issues and creating positive change. Natural Disasters. issues.tigweb.org/disasters

Understanding Katrina. understandingkatrina.ssrc.org

Organizations

Accord: Informing and Strengthening Peace Processes. www.c-r.org/our-work/accord/index.php?accser/series.htm

American Academy of Experts in Traumatic Stress. www.aaets.org

Amnesty International. Articles addressing the rights of refugees, indigenous communities, internally displaced communities and peoples, and international migrants. www.amnesty.org

Association for Women's Rights in Development. www.awid.org

Brookings Institution. Articles dealing with efforts to improve disaster planning and response by international organizations and governments. www.brookings.edu

Center for Disease Control and Prevention: Mental Health. www.bt.cdc.gov/mentalhealth

Center for Disease Control and Prevention: Wildfires. www.bt.cdc.gov/disasters/wildfires

Centre for Global Education. www.centreforglobaleducation.com

Columbia University. National Center for Disaster Preparedness. "The Legacy of Katrina's Children: Estimating the Numbers of Hurricane-related At-Risk Children in the Gulf Coast States of Louisiana and Mississippi." www.ncdp.mailman.columbia.edu/files/legacy_katrina_children.pdf

Columbia University. National Center for Disaster Preparedness. "The Recovery Divide: Poverty and the Widening Gap among Mississippi Children and Families Affected by Hurricana Katrina." www.ncdp.mailman.columbia.edu/files/recovery_divide.pdf

Foreign Policy Association. Great Decisions Blogs Archive: Children. children.foreignpolicyblogs.com/category/natural-disasters

Global Issues: Social, Political, Economic and Environmental Issues that Affect Us All. Section on Women's Rights. www.globalissues.org/article/166/womens-rights

Grameen Bank. www.grameen-info.org

Human Rights Watch. Articles dealing with children, international migration and internally displaced persons. www.hrw.org

Humanitarian Practice Network. www.odihpn.org

Inter-American Program on Education for Democratic Values and Practices. www.educadem.oas.org/english/cpo_links.asp

International Organization for Migration. www.iom.int

Johns Hopkins School of Public Health—Center for Refugee and Disaster Response. www.jhsph.edu/refugee/research/burma_cyclone/burma_cyclone.html

Mental Health America. Information on coping with disasters, particularly the impact on children. www.mentalhealthamerica.net

New York City Alliance Against Sexual Assault. Katrina Aftermath Fact Sheet. www.nycagainstrape.org/research_factsheet_111.html

Organization of American States: Inter-American Program on Education for Democratic Values and Practices. www.educadem.oas.org/english/cpo_links.asp

Save the Children Alliance. www.savethechildren.org

Save the Children—Sweden. Contains many publications dealing with issues of child protection during and after natural disasters employing a rights-based approach. www.scslat.org/eng/hacemos/2.php

United Nations. Human Development Reports. www.un.org

UNESCO. Social and Human Sciences—Human Rights—Children, Victims of War and Natural Disasters. www.unesco.org

United Nations High Commissioner for Refugees. Handbook for the Protection of Internally Displaced Persons. www.unhcr.org

UNICEF. Articles and podcasts on assisting children after natural disasters. www.unicef.org

University of California at Los Angeles. Center for Mental Health Studies in Schools. smhp.psych.ucla.edu

University of Illinois Extension—Disaster Resources. web.extension.uiuc.edu/disaster//teacher/teacher.html

University of Iowa Human Rights Center. Natural Disasters and Human Rights Impact. international.uiowa.edu/centers/human-rights/projects/human-rghts-index/13-2005.asp

U.S. Department of Health and Human Services. Hurricane Katrina website. www.hhs.gov/katrina

United States Institute of Peace. www.usip.org

Woodrow Wilson Center for Scholars. Beyond Disasters: Creating Opportunities for Peace. www.wilsoncenter.org/index.cfm?topic_id=1413&fuseaction=topics.event_summary&event_id=244464

Woodrow Wilson Center for Scholars. Environmental Change and Security Program. www.wilsoncenter.org/index.cfm?fuseaction=topics.home&topic_id=1413

EDITORS

Valerie Ooka Pang is a professor in the School of Teacher Education at San Diego State University. She has been the author and editor of many publications, including *Multicultural Education: A Caring-Centered, Reflective Approach* (McGraw-Hill, 2005 and Montezuma Publishing, 2nd edition, 2010) and *Struggling To Be Heard: The Unmet Needs of Asian Pacific American Children* (State University of New York Press, 1998). She was also general co-editor of the series *Race, Ethnicity, and Education*, and associate editor of *Theory and Research in Social Education* from 1998-2002. Her articles have appeared in a variety of journals, including *Harvard Educational Review, Phi Delta Kappan, Social Education, Theory and Research in Social Education*, and *The Journal of Teacher Education*. She was a senior Fellow for the Annenberg Institute for School Reform at Brown University and has been a consultant for organizations such as Sesame Street, Fox Children's Network, Family Communications (producers of Mr. Rogers' Neighborhood), and Scott Foresman.

William R. Fernekes is social studies supervisor at Hunterdon Central Regional High School in Flemington, NJ, a comprehensive suburban high school enrolling approximately 3,200 students. He supervises 30 full-time social studies faculty and oversees the social studies program, which received the NCSS Programs of Excellence award in 1997. He has published widely on the topics of social studies curriculum design, issues-based instruction, human rights education, and Holocaust and genocide studies. He serves as a consultant to the New Jersey Commission on Holocaust Education, and has authored two books: *Children's Rights: A Reference Handbook* (with Beverly Edmonds, ABC-CLIO, 1995) and *The Oryx Holocaust Sourcebook* (Greenwood Press, 2002). He is currently authoring a biography of the former U. S. Senator from New Jersey, Clifford P. Case II.

Jack L. Nelson, Professor Emeritus at Rutgers University, taught at elementary and secondary schools, and later at California State University, Los Angeles; SUNY Buffalo; and Rutgers. He has been a visiting scholar at Cambridge University, England; University of Sydney, and Curtin University, Australia; University of California, Berkeley; Stanford University; University of Colorado; and University of Washington in the U.S. The author or editor of 17 books and 175 other publications, his most recent book is *Critical Issues in Education*, co-authored with Stuart Palonsky and Mary Rose McCarthy. A recipient of the NCSS Academic Freedom Award, he continues to research and publish in his principal area of interest: advocacy for teacher and student freedoms.

AUTHORS

Thomas Chandler is a researcher at the National Center for Disaster Preparedness, Columbia University. He has also taught courses pertaining to geographic information systems (GIS) for the past five years at Teachers College, Columbia University. During 2007, Thomas worked as a curriculum developer for the Teaching The Levees curriculum project of Teachers College, which later became the focus of his doctoral dissertation, completed in 2009.

Margaret Smith Crocco is professor and coordinator of the Program in Social Studies and Chair of the Department of Arts and Humanities at Teachers College, Columbia University, where she has worked since 1993. She taught high school social studies for eight years. She has written widely on social studies education, with a particular interest in issues of gender and diversity. Her most recent book is *Clio in the Classroom: Teaching US Women's History*.

Angus M. Gunn is author of a number of books on education and environmental science. His main publications include: *High School Geography—Project Legacy; Habitat: Human Settlements in an Urban Age; The Impact of Geology on the United States*; and *Encyclopedia of Disasters: Environmental Catastrophes and Human Tragedies*.

Jeffrey W. Helsing is Deputy Director of the Domestic Education and Training programs at the United States Institute of Peace (USIP). He focuses on education in international relations, conflict resolution, human rights and peace studies. He has been part of the team responsible for the development of USIP's new Academy for Conflict Management and Peacebuilding, and has developed many of the Institute's faculty and teacher workshops as well as curriculum materials.

Walter Kälin is a Swiss legal scholar and professor of constitutional and international law at the Faculty of Law of the University of Bern. He has been closely concerned with issues of internally displaced persons for over a decade, and has authored numerous books on the subject, including the Annotations to the Guiding Principles. He was a member of the United Nations Human Rights Committee from 2003-2008, and served as the Special Rapporteur of the Commission on Human Rights on the situation of human rights in Kuwait under Iraqi occupation from 1991-1992.

Janet E. Lord is senior partner at BlueLaw International, LLP, a service-disabled, veteran-owned international law and development firm. She is an expert in international disability rights law and policy and has worked in more than 25 countries worldwide on disability inclusion in development programs. She participated in the negotiation of the UN Disability Convention and has taught international human rights law at the University of Maryland, American University and the University of Baltimore.

Merry M. Merryfield is professor in social studies and global education at The Ohio State University. She taught geography and African literature in Sierra Leone from 1977 to 1979 as a Peace Corps volunteer, and served as the outreach coordinator for the African Studies Program at Indiana University from 1981 to 1984. She was a Fulbright scholar researching social studies in Nigeria, Kenya, and Malawi in 1983-1985. In the late 1980s, she worked for USAID in Botswana as a technical specialist in curriculum development. She has written extensively about the role of social studies in national development in Africa.

Mavis B. Mhlauli is a doctoral candidate in the social studies and global education program at The Ohio State University. She is currently in Botswana collecting data on social studies teachers' conceptualizations and practice of education for global citizenship.

Marc A. Norman is an Associate Professor of Psychiatry at the University of California, San Diego. Dr. Norman is board certified in clinical neuropsychology from the American Board of Professional Psychology and is a Fellow of the National Academy of Neuropsychology. He has also been the chair and co-chair of Disaster Mental Health (DMH) for the American Red Cross San Diego/Imperial Counties Chapter, and a member of the American Red Cross's Critical Response Team. He has been deployed to numerous local, regional and national disasters.

Rick Oser is principal of an ethnically and linguistically diverse urban school in Lemon Grove, California. Formerly a special education teacher, Oser has worked as a principal with administrators, teachers, parents, and students during natural disasters that have affected schools. He has recently been awarded a grant of about $450,000 from the State of California to work on emotional, physical, and mental wellness in schools. In 2009, Oser was selected as Principal of the Year by the Governor's Council on Physical Fitness and Sports.

Bill Pisarra is a social studies teacher at Hunterdon Central Regional High School. The classes he teaches focus on world cultures, human rights, global security and geography. Pisarra took up teaching after a twenty-five year career as an executive in the software industry.

Mark A. Previte is an assistant professor of secondary education at the University of Pittsburgh at Johnstown. He is currently President of the Pennsylvania Council for the Social Studies, and the program chair for the National Council for the Social Studies Issues-Centered Education Community. He is a co-editor of the two-volume publication, *The NCSS Presidential Addresses: 1936-2000*.

Michael Ashley Stein is Executive Director of the Harvard Law School Project on Disability, a visiting professor at Harvard Law School, and Cabell Professor at William and Mary Law School. An internationally recognized disability rights expert, Professor Stein participated in the drafting of the United Nations Convention on the Rights of Persons with Disabilities, and actively consults with international governments on their disability laws and policies. He has taught at Harvard, New York University, and Stanford law schools.

Binaya Subedi is an assistant professor of social studies and global education at Ohio State University. He has written about topics that include prejudice, immigration, and race in journals such as *Social Education, Equity and Excellence in Education, Critical Inquiry,* and *Race, Ethnicity, and Education.* He is currently writing a book on the value of teaching and learning about critical global perspectives.

Felisa Tibbitts is co-founder and director of Human Rights Education Associates (HREA) and Adjunct Faculty at the United Nations' University for Peace and the Harvard Graduate School of Education. She has supported national curricular reform efforts in human rights, as well as law-related and civic education programming in many countries. She has served as a consultative expert for international organizations, including the ODIHR/OSCE, the Council of Europe, Office of the U.N. High Commissioner for Human Rights, Amnesty International, and the Organization of American States (OAS).

Bethany Vosburg-Bluem is a doctoral candidate in social studies and global education at The Ohio State University. Her interests include environmental education, the preparation of social studies teachers, and global education.

INDEX

V

W

Y

Z